Dedicated to the Noble Soul
who
possessed a firm mind
with
delicate heart
My brother
Mr. R. K. Singh (Dadda)

His blessings have always enlightened
my path.....

-D. K. Singh
Vice President
Heritage Institute of Hotel &Tourism
Agra

Economics of Hotel and Hospitality Management

D.K. Singh

Vice President
Heritage Institute of Hotel & Tourism
Agra

AMAN PUBLICATIONS
NEW DELHI

Published by
Rajiv Jain for Aman Publications
LG-4A, Ganpati Bhawan,
4675-B/21, Ansari Road,
Darya Ganj, Delhi - 110002
PH: 23255012, 23282127 -
E-mail: sshjbs@yahoo.com

First Published – 2007

ISBN–81–8204–041-8
        978-81–8204–041-0
© Publisher

SOLE DISTRIBUTOR
JINDAL BOOK SERVICES
LG-4A, Ganpati Bhawan,
4675-B/21, Ansari Road,
Darya Ganj, Delhi - 110002

Jacket Designed by :
S.M. Graphics

Printed by:
INDUS Press , Delhi, India

Preface

With unprecedented economic growth and resurgence in the tourism industry, hotel management has today come about to be a field which is closely monitored by many. In this area is an issue which is crucial to the way hotel management is practiced, the economic and finanacial management of a hotel.

Like corporate governance and management, the looking after of the financial sector is crucial to the management of a hotel enterprise. After all, finance and economics are the factors which fuel the running of this industry, just like almost every other business. The financial investment in a hotel determines how the hotel is perceived, and the cash flow and revenue is what makes that crucial difference between a booming business and bankruptcy. However, the specialization and the specifics of a hotel make it different from just any other form of a business venture, and therein lies the need for evaluating and assessing what entails the economic management of a hotel.

This book has been designed to serve as a one-step guide on effective economic and financial management of a hotel. Even as the duties of a hotel manager keep on becoming increasingly complex, the crucial aspect of finance cannot be ignored. Elucidating on the basic principles of good financial management, the book elaborates on what makes up the economics of a hotel, and how these principles can be applied to them. it also explains in-depth the economic factors which play the biggest role in the running of a hotel business, how relevant they are, how they should be managed, and how they could be improved upon. It also embarks upon an examination of the current trends and developments in this field. Erudite and insightful, it is hoped that the book fosters an enlightening reading experience.

Contents

Contents

1

Hotel Industry in New Economy

Since its beginning, the economy segment of hotel industry has undergone a continual process of transition. Although most owners, operators and lenders take a "stick to the basics" approach to economy lodging, a problem arises when one attempts to define just what "the basics" are. There are essentially two schools of thought when it comes to defining the basics. In the first, they revolve around price/value, guest satisfaction and market position; in the second, they focus on minimum amenities, minimum services and Spartan physical facilities. Although profitability is the goal of both approaches and both tend to focus on occupancy, the former group additionally recognizes that average daily rate (ADR) plays a role in the room-revenue formula.

These two approaches create a dynamic tension in the economy segment. This tension contributes to the excellent price/value that economy-hotel guests enjoy. The entry barriers to the economy segment are relatively low: Less than $2 million, with minimal equity requirements, will develop a very nice 40- to 50-room economy property. Don't scoff at that size, by the way: In many markets, it's just about right. Yes, the hotel will be fairly Spartan and yes, the owner will likely be a neophyte to the hotel industry. But that neophyte will learn in a few years what the old-time hotelier already knows: The mouse trap must be improved regularly if it's going to continue to work well.

As amenities and services are added, room rates must rise—but not beyond perceived value nor out of balance with the competitive market. Here is where the tension tightens: As soon as a new developer perceives an opening in the market and can obtain a secondary or tertiary site in a decent location, a new budget hotel appears on the scene. In response, management of the moderately priced hotel nearby moves to reposition it as an economy property by lowering rates. These two events create a market situation that's viewed as either highly competitive or overbuilt.

New amenities and services added to economy/limited-service properties to make them more competitive usually are inspired by their full-service big brothers. The constraints to adding new amenities are cost, staff and available land (or its marginal cost).

As a result, pools, hot tubs, and well-equipped exercise rooms have become almost commonplace in economy properties. Complimentary continental breakfasts, rather than just coffee and a doughnut, were adopted years ago from the all-suite model. Executive centers have appeared, complete with Internet access, fax machines, and copiers. Lobbies featuring couches, coffee tables and side chairs have replaced utilitarian entryways. When economy-hotel guests enter their room today, they expect to find Internet access, hair dryers, easy chairs, desks with large work surfaces, and remote-control cable TV with free movie channels. Even pay-per-view-movie firms, once reluctant to market their expensive installations to economy hotels, have discovered big profits in the segment's guestrooms.

Clearly, a significant number of investors believe that economy/limited-service hotels are more profitable than their full-service counterparts. All the statistics I've seen over the years support this premise as it relates to profit before income taxes as a percentage of sales. This is because the rooms department of any hotel, which is its very reason for existing, has the highest profit margin. Not only do the other revenue departments in full-service hotels have lower margins, but they also add undistributed expenses disproportional to their departmental margins. The question then becomes one of whether they add significantly to occupancy and ADR. It stands to reason, then, that operational profits as measured in cash flow are higher in full-service hotels, while the percentages are higher in economy/limited-service lodging properties.

The higher profit margins on sales would seem to imply that the economy/limited-service lodging hotel would have a higher degree of resiliency in down markets and quicker recovery as demand returns. The minimum staffing levels and other semi-fixed expenses necessary to maintain these hotels' service levels clearly set a very low floor on how much expense-cutting an operator can achieve once the variable expenses and value-added amenities have been cut in a depressed market. Because of the limited cash circulating through these properties, managers tend to be very conservative in their decisions regarding discretionary expense items, particularly in marketing and employee benefits.

Speaking of employees, labor costs in economy/limited-service lodging properties appear, on the surface, to be very low. With few exceptions, employee turnover is very high and is always blamed on local market conditions. The fact is that the typical manager has not been trained to check references, interview properly and effectively orient and train new employees. Often, the environment is such that the manager hires a "warm body" in hopes that the new employee will work out and the manager's own work load be reduced. The cycle, however, goes on as the new employee often becomes disenchanted and leaves. The hidden costs in poor efficiency and quality of work resulting from this system are obvious to all but the most unsophisticated — and could be corrected by more emphasis being placed on proper recruiting, interviewing, hiring and training procedures.

As for marketing, economy/limited-service hotels tend to focus on room rate and location. Due to the low payroll budgets, sales representatives are virtually unheard of in the segment — managers are expected to shoulder the burden of the direct-sales effort. Unfortunately, the typical economy-hotel manager defines "management" as getting reports done, hosting, and holding payroll to a minimum by working at the front desk for an inordinate amount of time. Competent training of staff, inspecting, civic involvement and quality sales calls are not commonly found in these properties. A major factor counteracting this tendency is the substantial support offered to operators by most franchisors in the economy segment. The top franchisors are getting more and more sophisticated in their marketing efforts. TV ads are becoming increasingly more effective, target marketing is implemented in very sophisticated ways, and any chain worth its salt has developed sophisticated Internet marketing and sales programmes.

IMPACTS OF GLOBALIZATION

In many countries, where tourism has become a major

export industry, the hospitality sector is the focal point for concepts of globalization to take root. Indeed, tourism has become the world¹s largest export industry, involving as it does enormous cross-border flows of people and capital. The hospitality industry is one of the world¹s largest employers and arguably one of the largest traders of foreign currency. It is often also a focal point for local society, and is clearly at the center of the transfer of ideas and the cross fertilization of cultures.

At its heart, the hospitality industry plays an important part physically in bringing people together in a global community. And those countries suffering from trade imbalances due to high imports frequently look to tourism and hospitality to close the gap. Hospitality is thus not only an industry, it is a concept — and a major force in the rapidly evolving global marketplace. The hospitality industry is thus at the very core of the globalization of international business. Hospitality companies therefore need to consider the implications of the global context in which they operate and must be prepared to address the questions that arise from this changing environment. What tangible trends driven by an inter-linked global marketplace will shape the hospitality industry of the future? What does globalization mean for the internationally oriented hospitality company, as well as hotel operations that compete locally and regionally with these organizations?

The globalization of business and lifestyles is characterized by communicating over vast distances in foreign languages, frequent travel to overseas countries, dealing in many currencies, and coping with a variety of political and social systems, regulatory environments, cultures and customs. While these aspects of globalization are easy to identify, understanding the underlying current and future trends can be problematic. Analysis, however, reveals that a number of issues are reshaping the global hospitality industry, although there are clearly some complex questions that are still to be resolved:

— International expansion with common product and brand position;

— Sales and marketing programmes that fully capture global economies of scale;

— Organizational structures that allow global delivery of services with local operational control;

— Cross-border employee training to support operations; and

— Use of the world capital markets as sources of funding.

Those hospitality companies that believe that they can grow and retain a niche position without acknowledging the imperatives of globalization need to take another look. Put another way, most hospitality businesses will need to think "globally" if they are to survive. That goes for organizations competing in the mature European and U.S. markets, which are now seeing stiff competition from other parts of the world, especially Asia. The sheer size of the vast U.S. market, in particular, can promote an insular point of view, but hotel companies that concern themselves only with the dynamics of this domestic arena also need to hear the "wake up" call.

Globalization will ultimately touch virtually all aspects of the hospitality industry. Increasingly, customers, management processes, employees, products, and sources of capital will be competed for and will move across national boundaries. Companies which are unprepared for this will be left behind. Local or regional entities may believe that globalization is not their concern. But that view is in error — competition in the future will come from global entities with the advantages that globalization brings.

Expansion of Hotel Markets

Globalization is a natural outgrowth of trends that have evolved during the past 50 years. International hotel chains were invented after World War II; they grew in the 1960s, and expanded greatly in the following two decades. Industry and economic trends in this decade have further propelled the growth of internationally-oriented hotel companies for a variety of reasons.

Severe overbuilding of hotel markets, particularly in the United States during the 1980s, halted new development almost entirely, while scarcity of growth and development opportunities in markets around the world has further supported the trend toward industry consolidation. Many companies committed to growth have found that opportunities in their back yards have been limited because of overbuilding, and they have been forced to look beyond mature domestic markets to offshore opportunities.

The pressures to expand beyond national boundaries have largely arisen from the need for growing hotel companies to reach 'critical mass'— the point at which a network of properties is sufficiently large to satisfy the travel needs of the hotel company's most valued customers. For different companies with varying products and locations, critical mass will vary in scope.

A hotel organization, for example, may reach a point in which there is no other viable option than to expand across national boundaries if it wishes to grow, achieve critical mass and benefit from the economies of scale that accompany it. If this is the case, leadership will need to recognize the imperative of organizing as a global company. As an example, consider an international hotel company that is well established in North America and Europe. In today's world market, company leadership may cast attention on the potential for moving into burgeoning Asia/Pacific markets to compete with established regional companies. Companies considering such strategic options can succeed against strong local and regional competitors only if they capitalize on the advantages derived from being a global company.

While the large international chains continue to expand on a global basis, there are in the United States a number of brand names that have yet to reach the critical mass required for marketing success. The question this presents to the industry can be stated simply. Will the demands of globalization encourage further consolidation as smaller companies that have not achieved critical mass are acquired or put out of business?

The need for hotel companies to achieve critical mass and the attendant economies of scale suggests that we will see a diminishing number of larger companies in the future as the imperatives of global expansion persist. Economies of scale are real, not imagined, and marketing on a global basis creates a significant competitive edge. It is certain that brands and products will be increasingly marketed on a truly global basis. Growth and development functions will thus become even more critical for those organizations that have not yet achieved critical mass.

For those companies pursuing a global strategy and accustomed to hotel management contracts, franchising relationships and non-recourse financing, significant adjustments will need to be made to the growth and development model. In a number of markets around the world, the bifurcation of ownership from management and management from marketing is a concept yet to achieve real maturity. The process that promotes these concepts is a slow one and global-minded companies will need to respond accordingly.

The differences in financing, owning, operating and marketing hotel properties will thus eventually narrow in a more global environment. The challenge for companies growing into markets where local partnerships and alliances are required for success will be to convince their foreign counterparts of the benefits of structures that have been successful in their home countries. A company going offshore with a business concept, however, cannot assume that it will be wholly accepted. Differences will gradually break down, but for the time being it may be necessary to adjust to local realities.

Global Brands and Products

Hospitality customers increasingly seek predictable services that support their ability to move quickly and easily around the world. Indeed, the businesses and lifestyles of these multi-cultural travelers have themselves been shaped by globalization. The concept of projecting single brands globally is thus alluring, as well as being fully within the grasp of many hospitality companies. Nevertheless, there continues to be uncertainty about the benefits of establishing a single-brand presence in a global marketplace, in contrast to responding to the unique conditions at the local level.

A number of international hotel companies have sought the economies of scale attendant to developing single brands and products, and providing them in a uniform fashion to as many markets around the globe as possible. A countervailing trend is that many people —

both tourists and business travelers — seek the unique qualities and customs of an individual locale. In response, some international hotel companies have tried to reflect local culture in the way their hotels are designed and operated.

This is clearly an arena in which there is no one right answer, but rather a balance of complex factors required. For example, there is a general consensus that "global travelers," who travel frequently whether for business or recreation, usually prefer a uniform product, because they want the convenience and comfort of predictability, and they demand a high level of service. Those who travel less frequently, but have a fairly high level of sophistication may avoid such dominant global brand and product concepts. A third group is looking for what they are accustomed to, and are attracted by brands they are familiar with; in essence, they prefer to stay in environments that reflect their home-based experience.

Customer expectations are related to the level of the product, and hotel products at the lower end of the spectrum tend to be easier to standardize globally, in part because these properties are more clearly defined by physical attributes, which can be duplicated. At the upper end of the product quality spectrum, customers seek subtle differences in services and quality, which are not easily replicated.

Organizational Strategies

For the larger well-established international hotel companies that have circled the world in the quest for new opportunity, globalization has been a strategic concept for a number of years. International hotel companies have had to confront virtually all of the issues facing global enterprises — and in many cases more.

Unlike a manufacturer with an overseas plant, for example, a hotel company must export its entire operating business to function in diverse cultural and geographic settings. Hotel companies must have the capability of establishing an entire business concept in dramatically different local environments.

As the new century approaches, formulating organizational structures that can integrate individual businesses in one seamless global structure will remain an on-going challenge. Information technology clearly is one major factor shaping the opportunities for how global hotel companies organize themselves, offering the ability to communicate with customers electronically and linking far-flung operations.

It is also clear that global organizations also benefit by becoming flatter, in contrast to pyramid-shaped structures with strong central authority. Such decentralized organizations can narrow the distance (both physical and emotional) between employers and employees, at the same time putting management and staff closer to the customer.

Organizational structures that are based on hierarchical systems with authority centralized at a headquarters location, as a result, may be increasingly obsolete because they distance management from the customer, while at the same time failing to empower line management and staff responsible for delivering services. Fortunately, "flatter" and more decentralized organizations are greatly facilitated by the increasing sophistication of technology and communications.

In addition, hotel company employees represent a melting pot of cultures, customs and languages, requiring new visioning and management skills to manage effectively, as well as a commitment to education and training that is unprecedented in its breadth. Today's hotel schools will need to increase their focus on issues that have to do with a global environment — communications, international marketing and law, history, social studies, geography and language. Company-wide training in a global organization to assure consistent leadership, operational skills and service delivery also represents a considerable challenge.

All of these factors suggest that companies expanding globally can benefit greatly by forming strategic alliances. A number of companies are moving towards such alliances with regional partners as a key strategy to provide entry to new and relatively unfamiliar markets and assure a higher level of local knowledge. Going it alone is increasingly expensive and frequently more risky. Substantial sums of money can be spent trying to conquer a region, and there may be considerable wisdom in forging alliances with local and regional partners. Foreign hotel groups have long found it difficult to establish a U.S. presence and distribution system, for example, and will probably need to enter into alliances, rather than establishing a new product from the ground up in an extremely competitive market.

At their best, alliances capitalize on the strengths of large, multinational corporations while drawing on the benefits that tend to accrue to smaller, more differentiated companies. Creating an integrated organization from such alliances presents a challenge, however. The overriding issue operationally is how best to maintain a firm, fixed center while encouraging flexibility and proactive approaches to local conditions. Also at issue is the choice of partner. Here, a shared operational philosophy and product/customer orientation are mandatory if the combined whole is to become bigger and more successful than the sum of the parts.

Operational Paradox

A recurrent issue for hotel companies in a global context is the need to develop global brands and image, while at the same time empowering management and staff closest to the customer in day-to-day operations. On the one hand, decentralized structures allow a hotel company to give authority to employees at the property level. Once the customer walks in the door, the service is controlled and delivered at the local level — with virtually no headquarters interface, even if those services have been centrally designed. But a key — and potentially controversial — question arises. Are chain and operational economies of scale thus increasingly irrelevant in a global context involving greater decentralization?

Customers want to be served locally in the hotels they patronize. But they want to make reservations and communicate electronically on the Internet — pointing to a bifurcation of the economies of scale possible in a global organization between marketing and operations. While operational issues must be dealt with locally, marketing is very much a corporate, chain-wide function that lends itself to realizing the benefits of global structures. As a result, it is possible that the economies of scale that can be achieved by a global organization may have less to do with operations — the running of a hotel — and much more to do with marketing.

Companies need to resolve this seeming paradox. They will need to secure a balanced position between these two objectives, which are potentially conflicting — decentralization for operational needs while taking advantage of global structures in the marketing arena. One might conclude that it will be marketing-driven organizations, especially franchisors with strong brand names, that are better able to capitalize on globalization and its communications benefits than those companies that persist in operating from a centralized base. For forward-looking companies, headquarters must be viewed not as a physical place but a dynamic function that exists either electronically or in person wherever it is needed. The 'marketplace' has become the 'marketspace'.

As hospitality companies grow into the global economy, they will need to look to global capital markets for support. Investment capital, however, continues to be in short supply and this situation will continue for some time. Companies that wish to attract investors will need to demonstrate that they can offer better returns and performance than in the past. And, at least in the eyes of the world's financial markets, they will need to demonstrate their viability as companies in a global marketplace.

For the first time real estate is now being traded as a commodity in securities markets, and we can therefore expect hospitality products in the future to be viewed in the same manner. The securitization of real estate in the United States represents a significant trend, and it behooves savvy futurists to track these trends as they develop elsewhere in the world.

Indeed, the world's financial markets are at the cutting edge of globalization, driven by the revolution in communications. With investment portfolios passed between the Americas, Europe and Asia/Pacific in a time continuum without interruption, 24-hour financial markets are here and are destined to impact significantly the way their customers use them. Hospitality companies that seek capital from the public marketplace will need to function as global enterprises. If the public markets on a global basis are going to serve corporations and produce optimum results, those public companies that feed into any or all of the three major financial centers of the world (New York, Tokyo, and London) need to view themselves and to be viewed as global enterprises in order to benefit fully from what these markets have to offer.

Hospitality companies that want to trade in the financial markets will need a business concept that is relatively easy to communicate and comprehend. Those companies that provide homogeneity in products and market orientations will be the most attractive to global capital markets. Companies with simple and well-defined products such as Coca Cola have become recognized by customers and investors around the world. Hospitality companies that want to trade in the financial markets will need a business concept that is relatively easy to communicate and comprehend. A truly global enterprise will have the ability to react quickly to market opportunities, no matter where they present themselves by applying business concepts that have been proven in the context of a global undertaking.

Role of Mobile Executives

Globalisation brings new challenges to the hospitality and leisure industries, which are under increasing pressure to serve international business and tourism markets worldwide. Experienced hotel and leisure industry executives have often been transferred outside their home countries, whether to new build locations, new acquisitions or to enhance the provision of services of an existing operation. With the evolution of a global marketplace, attitudes toward assignments out of the home country, as well as provision for compensation and benefits, have shifted significantly in the hospitality and leisure industries. For the truly mobile executive, the strongest development route may now be through a variety of international assignments with that individual bearing some of the "cost" of the assignment in return for stronger career development prospects.

To retain and motivate executives accepting assignments outside the home country, it is important to remunerate them accordingly. Nevertheless, payroll and related costs often account for as much as 45-60 percent of hotel expenses, and it is crucial that the costs of such transfers be controlled. In addition, new and more flexible approaches to compensating those executives accepting overseas assignments are evolving to match the needs of companies and employees in a global economy.

The traditional approach to compensating executives transferred from home countries in the past involved a central assumption - executives will be reluctant to take on an overseas assignment, and therefore the process should be as painless as possible. The so-called Balance Sheet approach has broadly aimed to maintain the individual's home country spending power in the new host country.

Once an individual with the requisite expertise was identified and the family/personal issues were resolved, the company developed a package to ensure the individual was not adversely affected financially by the assignment. The individual's basic pay was augmented with additional entitlements or allowances to cover the following:

— Cost of living (COLA);

— Expatriate premium;

— Housing;

— Education (for individuals with families);

— Home leave;

— Professional tax advice; Tax protection/tax equalisation.

When possible and practical, an individual generally continues to pay contributions to social security, pension schemes, and life and medical coverage in the home country. As a result, if the individual is transferred to a country or area with a high cost of living or a more costly taxation regime, providing a remuneration package can prove to be very expensive.

The Balance Sheet approach is relatively easy to understand, reduces suspicion that the executive is being disadvantaged, and by virtue of the fact that the executive is well remunerated, aids mobility. In addition, however, it can be:

— Expensive for the employer;

— Focused on the net benefit to the employee rather than driving down costs for the employer;

— Probably outdated as employers move to a global approach.

To ensure that the employee is not financially worse off, tax equalisation and protection schemes are often adopted. In a tax equalisation scheme, a hypothetical amount of home country tax is calculated on the usual elements of compensation (i.e. excluding extra amounts received as a result of the assignment). The employer withholds the hypothetical tax while paying the actual tax liabilities to the employee's home and host countries. There is often an extra cost associated with this payment of an employee's tax liability by the employer, as this generally creates further taxable income, and therefore there is a tax on tax or 'gross up' effect. At the end of the year the final hypothetical tax liability is calculated and any under-, or over-payment of hypothetical tax is paid by, or reimbursed to, the employee. Consequently, the executive who has been transferred is no better or worse off than before the assignment. Any benefits arising from tax planning within these schemes are benefits to the company.

With a tax protection scheme the employee is responsible for actual tax and social security liabilities in both the home and overseas countries. These liabilities are then compared to the liability that would have risen had the assignment not taken place and any additional tax costs are reimbursed on a grossed-up basis. As a result, the employee cannot be worse off, but may receive a tax windfall if the actual costs are lower than they would have been in the employee's home country.

Net pay schemes are also a common feature of such assignments. Hypothetical tax and social security is calculated dependent upon an individual's salary, family size and other factors. The individual's pay, net of this amount, is guaranteed. The employer then assumes responsibility for all actual tax liabilities which are paid on a grossed-up basis. Usually net pay is also augmented by allowances for the individual. An advantage of this method is that no year-end reconciliation is needed as the net pay is guaranteed beforehand.

Tax protection or equalisation in a high tax environment can be very expensive for the employer. Planning an assignment, therefore, is crucial to reducing the associated costs as far as possible. Much can be done to limit the impact of taxes, including:

— Taking advantage of potential tax treaty exemptions. This may require consideration of the number of days spent in the foreign country, and who should be the employer or who should bear the employee's costs.

— Qualifying as a non-resident in years of arrival and departure, and consequently being taxed at a lower rate or not taxed at all. Timing here can be crucial.

— Maximising advantages of graduated tax rates.

— Delivering related allowances as cost effectively as possible. For example, home country social security costs may be saved if a portion of the allowance is paid by the employer as a direct payment to a third party for services such as housing. This is in contrast to providing a cash allowance to the employee, which would be subject to social security contributions.

— Using opportunities such as separate employment arrangements and special premiums for work outside the foreign country.

Pensions are another important area for consideration to ensure that pension contributions/coverage are not disrupted. For a short-term assignment an employee generally would continue contributing to his or her home country scheme. However, this may not necessarily be the most tax efficient planning for an individual on a longer term assignment, who possibly may not return to the home country. A solution adopted in the hotel sector involves establishing a worldwide unapproved plan to prevent employees accumulating limited pension entitlements in several locations. In this case, the benefits of maintaining one single fund outweigh the reduced tax efficiency.

Inheritance or estate taxes are frequently overlooked when planning an assignment. Generally employers will pay for professional advice in resolving complications with overseas and home country taxes as a result of an employee's death during his or her time away from the home country. This can prove costly to an employer and stressful to the family, so the following should be considered in advance:

— Does a tax treaty exempt the employee from taxes in the host country?

— Has the employee a valid will for both countries?

Globalisation puts considerable pressure on human resource personnel to re-evaluate the traditional methods of providing for executive assignments and to develop innovative new packages suitable for the globalised economy. This represents an increased challenge to human resource personnel during a time when head counts for support functions are under scrutiny.

In addition to the traditional expatriate moving to a specific assignment country and back, typically with a specific technical skill, there is a new breed of mobile executive who has no home country, but rather moves from location to location with career progression a primary motivator. For the latter, a single rigid policy covering different types of employees will be ineffective, and a more flexible, global policy is required.

Expatriate assignments also are becoming longer-term because of changes in the business environment. Such expatriates may have adapted to the host country way of life, and as the employer has made the up-front investment in transferring the individual overseas, a solution needs to be identified to phase the individual onto local terms and conditions. The key to a successful transition will be the presentation of the reasons and methodology of the transition policy to the individual in a way which is easily understood and accepted.

It is likely that the Balance Sheet approach will soon be outdated as a general method for dealing with international transfers. Despite its popularity, fairness of treatment and logical approach, it is becoming too expensive for the employer to assume tax protection/ equalisation. Furthermore, using general assumptions to calculate the allowances for transferred individuals is often not the most appropriate way to determine benefits. It does not provide an incentive to drive down costs; perhaps most importantly, it lacks the flexibility required in today's global economy to enable the package to be tailored to meet individual circumstance and requirements.

The move to a global policy for international transfers requires a fundamental re-evaluation of the compensation and benefits approach. Pay and benefits will need to be re-engineered, with a system to differentiate high performance individuals and which reduces the importance placed on the pure money aspects of the pay and benefits package. This is not, however, going to be all bad news for the mobile executive; to date, this individual may not have extracted maximum value out of the assignment package.

The future will see the introduction of more flexible packages of benefits to meet the personal objectives of the individual. Rather than having fixed housing and schooling allowances, for example, an overall price might be put on the remuneration package so the individual can choose how that package is made up and used. In essence, the individual will be able to pick from a menu of benefits and design the package which is most appropriate to specific needs and aspirations. This menu, of course, must have tax considerations incorporated into the design so that the concept of gain sharing (sharing planning benefits between employer and executive) can be used to obtain the employee's buy-in and assistance in developing the benefits which will be offered. Such an approach would be weighted for different assignment locations to take account of local cost differentials.

COMMODITIZATION OF HOTEL PRODUCTS

Commoditization of hotel product has occurred over the past eleven years or so, largely because of the unprecedented price transparency brought on by the Internet and the unhealthy industry practices of competing online on price and price alone. In addition, third-party online intermediaries and their price-focused marketing initiatives have been responsible for the further commoditization of hotel products and services.

Here are several important developments in distribution in hospitality that have contributed one way or another to commoditization of the hotel product:

— The shift from GDS, call center, and the offline channel to Internet Distribution, which means a shift toward complete price transparency and easy "shopping around" of hotel rates and offerings.

— Working with third-party online intermediaries that propagate the Web with price-driven hotel offers.

— Rate Parity across all distribution channels has become the industry norm over the last 5 years. Though a highly positive move aimed to prevent price erosion, rate parity has contributed to the commoditization of the hotel product and services.

— Best Internet Rate Guarantee has become the industry norm—this is good news. The bad news is that every player in the industry offers best rate guarantees, and this marketing aspect has stopped being a differentiating factor.

— Matching the rates of the hotel's comp set has become the industry norm. Rate comparison reports provide a quick snapshot of the hotel comp set's current, 30- and 60-day out rates, so maintaining this "comp set rate consistency" has never been easier.

Just imagine how the hotel world looks through the eyes of the average travel consumer:

— You find practically the same rates for comparable hotels (same room type/stay period) in any destination

— You find the same rates for the same hotel (same room type/stay period) if you research the hotel's own website.

Under the scenario described above, how would the average travel consumer select a hotel? Obviously, additional factors play in the property selection process:

— Familiarity with the property (i.e. return guests, family and friend referrals, etc.)

— Brand recognition (i.e. strength of the brand, etc.)

— Customer retention programmes in place (i.e. reward programmes). Loyalty programmes are very popular with travelers and especially with people who book online.

— Last, but not least, the "value proposition" of a particular hotel or hotel offering. This is the most important single factor to facilitate the decision process.

Brand enhancement and appealing customer retention programmes are expensive, long-term objectives. Providing unique value proposition to the potential customer and differentiating your hotel product from what the competition is offering are much easier initiatives to implement.

De-Commoditization Strategy

A comprehensive de-commoditization strategy has the important goal of providing a unique value proposition to hotel customers. This strategy identifies unique aspects of a hotel product and destination, and develops a differentiated approach to a hotel's key customer segments. This strategy allows hoteliers to create unique specials and packages, event-related getaways, seasonal promotions, and launch marketing initiatives that provide unique value to the customer.

A robust de-commoditization strategy involves the following:

— Focus on the value side of the Price vs. Value Equation
— Differentiation of the hotel product offering from offerings by the comp set
— Differentiation of the hotel offering from the indirect channels (i.e. third-party online intermediaries)
— Differentiated approach to the hotel's different key customer segments.

Value vs. Price Equation

Focusing on the price side of the Value vs. Price Equation is the main driver toward commoditization in the hotel industry. What should hoteliers do to change the current situation?

— Stop competing on price only. Hoteliers will never be able to attract and retain more sophisticated travel shoppers and more affluent customers if they compete on price alone.
— Re-focus the hotel product offering and marketing on the value side of the Value vs. Price Equation.
— When designing the hotel marketing strategy, create unique hotel offers based on unique product attributes and attributes in the local environment.
— Create distinctive product offerings designed to provide a unique value proposition to your hotel

customers, such as suite specials and romantic getaways to boost sales of suites and hotel packages such as family packages, weekend getaways, museum packages, seasonal packages, golf packages, and spa packages, to name a few.

De-Commoditization Tool

Travel consumers look for product uniqueness, special opportunities and value. Creating unique specials and packages, event-related getaways, seasonal promotions and other marketing initiatives that provide unique value to the customer should become an important aspect of the hotelier's de-commoditization strategy.

A hotel special offer or promotion creates not only strong value proposition to potential customers, but a highly marketable product the hotel can now promote via search marketing, email marketing, online sponsorships and display advertising, and in the print media.

SHARED SERVICES

The traditional hotel company, comprised of owned, managed, and franchised properties has historically located accounting and finance employees at the property level, as well as at the corporate office. Traditionally all financial information has been sent to the corporate office for consolidation; data analysis and reporting, although the primary processing has taken place at the property level. Often, the different systems being used at the individual hotels have resulted in inefficiencies at the corporate level with many manual processes being required, including data re-entry, in order to complete a consolidation and prepare the necessary executive information. The relatively antiquated and cumbersome information systems at the corporate headquarters have further hindered the ability of users to receive information in a timely and cost-efficient manner.

A number of the major hotel companies are either considering or are already moving towards implementation of a shared services system. Factors driving this decision include a desire for growth, the need to outperform the competition, and the desire to satisfy both the company's guests and individual hotel owners. All of these factors - coupled with a need to reduce overhead costs - makes shared services a viable solution. The shared services model can help to lower processing costs, create a customer-driven "center of excellence," consolidate multiple processing locations into one location and incorporate a "fee for service" approach to transaction processing. This model is geared towards repetitive transactions that can be somewhat automated or handled through mass processing. Personnel can be consolidated and spend more time on "value-added" tasks under this model. Management will then be able to spend more time on making informed decisions, as meaningful data will be more readily available.

Centralization

Centralization, however, introduces several new business challenges which must be addressed prior to implementing a shared services system, with the selection of current technology to support a new structure being one of the most important. The many pieces in the technology puzzle include the architecture required to support the central functions, the application software needed to best handle data processing and reporting, and the communication requirements between the service center and remote locations. Each site will need its own Local Area Network (LAN), which will then be connected to the Wide Area Network (WAN). The WAN will connect all remote sites to the central service center, and the central service center to the corporate headquarters if they are separated geographically, and allow users to access data for the entire enterprise as appropriate. To access the data, communication lines from each remote site to the service center database will need to be in place.

The application software is also very important in the infrastructure of the service center. It needs to be functionally rich and powerful enough to handle processing and reporting for multiple entities which may have very different requirements. For example, a resort hotel may need to track more detail than a small hotel with no restaurants, and institutional owners may need different reports than a developer/owner. The system must track an abundance of information, but also be capable of segregating the information so that management can access only the key results they need. Management must have extensive on-line data access and reporting tools to assist them in decision-making and business planning.

Within the technology challenge, system security becomes an issue. When accounting functions including payables and receivables are being processed by a service center which is handling numerous owner's accounts, data integrity becomes a primary concern. A system needs multiple levels of security to ensure that data is secured, that appropriate access is granted only to the people who should handle the data and that audit trails are available for researching any discrepancies.

Assessing Costs and Savings

Possibly the biggest challenge in centralizing transaction processing is determining the costs and savings from creating a shared service structure. Costs can range from new hardware and software purchases to relocation costs of employees reassigned to work in the service center. The costs must be allocated to those who will benefit from and receive services from the new center. The costs for the shared services model are easier to identify than the savings. The initial investment in the service center includes:

— Application hardware and software;
— The WAN and LAN costs;
— Rent and building improvements;
— Employee relocation and severance expense;
— Initial training and change management;
— Implementing the new structure.

The on-going costs include the training and procedure development, communication costs, payroll and other overhead expenses.

The benefits of a service center are more difficult to assess than the costs as many are intangible, including the potential for providing easier access to more meaningful data. A shared service center also may result in more informed decision-making and an infrastructure capable of supporting increased growth. Placing a dollar value on such benefits can be difficult. Other benefits, however, can be more readily quantified, including:

— Reduced total head count;
— Processing time per transaction;
— Improved customer service response times;
— Improved average days to collect outstanding receivables.

Depending on the current environment and the number of repetitive tasks, the savings will vary. Companies that depend on manual processing or have outdated information systems can realize the greatest savings. Companies that have numerous locations that handle the same types of transactions can also realize big savings.

Economically, the shared services model can work. Initial investments can be allocated on a pro-rata share basis to each participating location. Ongoing costs can also be allocated based either on a "fee-for-service" basis or a flat annual fee. Along with the savings, these allocations make the centralization structure a cost reduction tool for many organizations.

Change Management

Companies adopting a centralized process structure under a shared service model often implement change management efforts along with new information systems. Together, the two initiatives create an environment for reducing operating costs and improving efficiencies. In developing a strategy for a shared service center, a phased approach is preferable. The first phase calls for a Conference Room Pilot (CRP), which involves a minimal set-up of the new hardware and software at corporate headquarters, and one or two remote properties brought on line to test the entire design. Corporate implementation is followed by the second phase, the enterprise-wide roll-out.

The CRP phase is designed to identify unique requirements and assess the risks associated with the service center concept. Detailed requirements, confirmation and design will be completed during this phase. The technical architecture will be implemented, selected business scenarios tested and change management efforts developed during the CRP. As part of the change management efforts, all newly centralized processes will be redefined. Workflow will be streamlined and current job descriptions will be revamped while new job descriptions are being defined.

During the next phase, Service Center Implementation, change management and process improvement implementation efforts will be the main focus. Newly defined processing methods will be implemented. All remaining untested business scenarios will be tested. Data conversion and testing will take place. The center will then go online and processing will begin. The next phase, Remote Location Implementation, will consist of the same implementation efforts from the previous phase, but will focus on the individual hotels. During this phase, an implementation team approach will be utilized. Small, highly focused teams will go to each remote location to quickly implement the centralized structure and bring them up on the new system. Change management will also be very important as the move to a shared service center often results in significant changes in the way the accounting and finance function is conducted at the hotel. In particular, the role of the hotel controller will likely undergo major change.

All locations need to be involved in the process of developing and implementing a shared service center. This was the most valuable lesson learned during the analysis of centralization versus decentralization in information processing. Determining what functions to handle at the local level - in contrast to the service center - was one of the most difficult tasks. Without assistance from the individual locations, decisions would be made in a vacuum reflecting only the perspective of the corporate headquarters. To be successful, organizations need early buy-in from both management and staff personnel in all areas within the company. The more involved each project team member is, the smoother and more valuable the transition will be. Clearly, hotel companies need to review their operations as they seek to manage properties better, cheaper and more efficiently. The shared services model offers great potential, particularly for large hotel companies with operations scattered across distant locations. Cost savings from more efficient transaction processing can be significant, freeing capital currently used in "back-office" operations for other purposes, including strategic growth.

RATE SETTING CHALLENGES

Each industry is struggling with managing group rates; all are working to understand how to keep promotions from cannibalizing current offerings; and in each market shoppers are price sensitive because of the Internet, seasonality and other outside factors. Now several hotel companies are looking over the fence and boosting their bottom lines by applying successful revenue management strategies modeled from other industries.

The key to doing this is a thorough understanding of the buying dynamics and influences in a number of industries. With its experience in service- and product-based markets supporting Fortune 1,000 clients, Manugistics has identified several revenue management best-practice areas from other industries that it is leveraging for hospitality chains.

We discovered three rate-setting challenges common to retailers, delivery companies, consumer electronics chains and hotel companies. Each organization is:

— Creating group rate strategies in a highly competitive market;

— Working to avoid cannibalization of existing pricing by new rate offerings; and

— Adapting flexible pricing to fluctuating demand.

Additionally, Internet usage is putting the same downward pricing pressure on these companies – just like hospitality. By modeling the market dynamics for a U.S. auto retailer and a United Kingdom-based grocery chain, for instance, Manugistics was able to test different influences and accurately predict how they affected demand. The result is a set of robust, flexible revenue maximization solutions from other industries, which can be applied to hotel chains that need to optimize revenue. Here is a closer look at the common challenges that can be solved with this approach.

Group Pricing

Group pricing optimization is one of the most complex calculations for hotel chain revenue management directors. Before they can generate a proposal for group business, managers must accurately forecast sleeping room pick-up, food and beverage revenue, meeting space value, incidental spending, and the value of possible future client business. Based on these estimates they need to deliver a bid low enough to win the business against competing hotels, but high enough to maximize profitability. They must also balance all of these considerations against the potential value of other groups requesting the same dates and space. This is similar to the auto industry. When a customer requests a block of units, let's say 50 yellow cabs or police cars, managers need to know how much to offer so that the chance of winning the deal is very high. Bids must consider the mix of sedans, mid-sized vehicles or minivans, the accessories that are requested, how long the account has been buying from the manufacturer and what other manufacturers are submitting.

Promotions Forecasting

Short-term promotions that cannibalize higher rated offerings is another problem that confronts nearly all industries. We gained valuable understanding of the relationship between price and demand from our work maximizing promotional revenue for a large United

Kingdom-based grocery chain. Before you say that retail is nothing like the hospitality business, consider that when a retail store discounts pricing on a brand of cereal, it cannibalizes the sale of similar higher-priced products. In Hospitality, Internet discounting cannibalizes higher room rates for nearly every property.

Price Sensitivity

For hotel operators the crucial question is not if ADR will be lowered by Internet discounts, but at what price point the downward movement will begin. By employing sophisticated price-elasticity modeling, we learned to predict buyer price sensitivity in many industries including consumer electronics.

Now we are using that knowledge to build pricing strategies that synchronize rates with promotions for hotel operators. What makes the hotel industry unique is that rate analysis must go beyond pricing because guests often contribute considerable incidental revenue and may represent repeat business. What is the lifetime value of a guest? To what extent should a hospitality company reduce their room rate to account for the fact that a guest has been loyal in the past?

An extreme example would be gaming companies, who not only reduce the room rate to zero, but upgrade the suite for their best guests. Rate optimization modules predict guest spending in a flexible framework to forecast total guest revenue for any type of property, full- or limited-service, luxury to budget. The result is a system that predicts a promotion's total revenue impact on guest value at multiple price points under varying conditions.

2

Financing of Hotel Development

Public sector support for hospitality development has been episodic and erratic as economic development policies have shifted. When government has commonly stepped in, support has focused on the development of key hotel properties deemed essential to stimulate business travel and tourism, and create new jobs. Formal public/private alliances in these cases have often opened the door to lower-cost financing of hotel development, as well as a host of other incentives to stimulate private investment.

Public entities have at their disposal a wide array of programmes and financial vehicles that can assist in making a hotel project feasible and thus contribute to an area's overall economic well-being. The potential to access lower-cost financing, tap redevelopment incentives, structure favorable land lease terms, secure site improvements and other alternatives should not be overlooked by hotel developers when development projects have a clear link to public interests.

Public financing of private hotel investment is not new. The Small Business Administration (SBA) of US, for example, has financed the development of smaller hotels since the mid 1950s. In the past four years, loans provided by the SBA for hotels were approximately three percent of total SBA loans, and the average size was $560,000. Most commonly, however, public financing and other incentives to promote hospitality investment in the United States have arisen at the local level in development of convention headquarters hotels, which are essential to the success of these large meeting and trade show facilities. Conventions are big business in the United States with more than 800,000 national meetings held annually, much of that market dominated by corporate bookings. Collectively, these conventions attracted some 55 million attendees in 1993.

The more than 500 public and private convention and meeting centers in the United States, in fact, typically form a linchpin in the economic development strategies of local and regional governments. Convention center development and expansion have been components of local economic development strategies since the mid-1980s and continue to rise. Three new centers opened in the last 18 months at locations in Charlotte, North Carolina; Mobile, Alabama; and outside Washington, D.C. And a 1994 Tradeshow Week survey indicated that more than 60 percent of U.S. convention centers were considering expansion — versus only 31 percent in 1993. Planned expansions of exhibition space in convention centers are expected to generate 58.8 million square feet as of 1994, climbing to 64 million by 1999.

The interdependent economics of convention centers and the hotels that serve them create opportunities for public/private partnerships of benefit to government entities and private investors. The evolution of public/private partnerships to support development of convention headquarters hotels, as a result, offer an excellent foundation for examining how public sector financing and other incentives can support private hotel investment.

Most cities require a convention headquarters hotel to market their convention center successfully. Yet many mid- to upper-tier cities often lack sufficient hotel inventory that can be specifically committed to this purpose. Conversely, room nights generated from a convention center are often insufficient to exclusively support a convention headquarters hotel serving the meetings and trade shows so important to local economies. Further complicating the problem, convention headquarters hotels often incur higher than typical development costs due to the amount and quality of public areas required. The result — a need for public/ private partnerships to support the economic feasibility of a convention headquarters hotel. This hotel, in turn, will support the public investment made in a convention center, as well as generating other local economic benefits.

These public/private partnerships have therefore become increasingly critical as convention center facilities have proliferated in the United States. They also evidence the range of options available to the public sector to support private hotel development. While these types of incentives most often may be used to support convention hotels, they may also be important tools for other types of hotel projects in which there is a strong relationship between public interests and private investment.

Nearly 65 percent of U.S. convention centers are owned by cities, counties, states or other types of government authorities. Major convention cities, such as New York or Las Vegas, generally have had sufficient hotel supply in appropriate locations to support the needs generated by meeting and trade show participants. For many other municipalities, however, new hotel development can be critical to competing for the middle- to upper-tier convention market. Convention facilities in these cities may be located in areas peripheral to hotel concentrations. In addition, existing hotel operators are often reluctant to commit the room inventory required to serve convention delegates — typically offered in package deals at lower room rates — while simultaneously reducing rooms available to serve guests that make up their core business.

The basic economics in hotel development and operations pose additional challenges. Convention-oriented hotels are typically 10 to 20 percent more expensive to develop than a comparable size, group-oriented hotel. At the same time, room rates for a convention hotel's core market segment may run 20 to 30 percent below comparable business hotels due to discount package deals negotiated for delegates as part of convention attendance. To remain successful, a convention center must attract annual national bookings in the range of 25 to 30 events that have a minimum of 2,500 participants each. These bookings, however, on average support occupancies of only 30 to 35 percent in terms of total room nights. As a result of these factors, convention center hotel properties must either achieve higher average occupancies, develop other sources of business or realize higher room rates attributable to non-convention guests to succeed.

Convention hotels can often attract alternative sources of revenue, including sponsoring convention and meeting trade separate from a convention center. Sources of business may include smaller group business, commercial activity, and wholesale and tour operator business. Nevertheless, the hotel is in most cases fundamentally dependent on the convention center for its core business.

To entice new development, local government entities must often work jointly with hotel developers to overcome the obstacles that tend to make these hotels more costly to develop and less profitable to operate.

PUBLIC/PRIVATE PARTNERSHIPS

These issues raise critical questions. What tools can government bring to bear to attract private hotel investment by improving their economics? How can a hotel developer work with local governments to close the economics gap and make development feasible? Initiatives prior to the 1986 Tax Reform Act pointed the way to creative forms of public/private partnerships serving the interests of convention centers and their headquarters hotels. The City of Miami, for example, provided an array of incentives to attract hotel development in support of the James I. Knight Center. The city acquired land, provided a 45-year lease with attractive terms and furnished off-site improvements, as well as site utilities. The hotel additionally was awarded the food & beverage concession for the convention center, and real estate property taxes were abated during construction.

The incentives provided by the City of Toledo at Seagate Center is another case in point. A $7.4 million Urban Development Action Grant was loaned to the developer through the Convention Bureau at attractive rates and terms. Tax increment financing was used to support public improvements, while real estate taxes were abated. In addition, the hotel was supplied with convention center-owned parking at prevailing market rates.

More recent public/private partnership successes include the Westin Hotel venture in Providence, Rhode

Island, which involved a $290 million bond issue, that covered the convention center, hotel and parking. A Sheraton Hotel at the Jefferson Center in Birmingham, Alabama, involved a $148 million low-interest bond offering, guaranteed by JCA and supported by city and county occupational taxes.

Not all public/private partnerships come together, despite concerted efforts on the part of both private developers and public entities. In Tampa, studies indicated a strong need for a convention hotel to support the city's new convention center. A city commission approved a proposed 900-room Marriott hotel, estimated to cost more than $140 million or more, and to be owned by a private 'not for profit' corporation. Public financing for the hotel, however, was rejected by the Tampa City Council last year. A special task force spent six months analyzing two options and is presently formulating recommendations.

The dilemma faced in Los Angeles also is a case in point. A major expansion of the Los Angeles Convention Center was completed late last year, increasing total meeting space to more than 600,000 square feet. Historically, however, the center has hosted only about 20 conventions annually, and competition from other Western cities — including San Francisco, San Diego, Anaheim, Long Beach, Seattle, Portland and Las Vegas — has become more intense.

The Los Angeles Convention and Visitors Bureau has contended that a convention hotel within walking distance is required to make the city more competitive for attracting large conventions. Yet the downtown Los Angeles hotel market has been weak since the onset of the recession early in this decade, a condition which has been further exacerbated by the Los Angeles riots in 1992 and the Northridge earthquake last year. Downtown's primary convention hotels, all located within seven blocks of the convention center, collectively posted occupancies in the mid-50 percent range last year (up more than six occupancy points from one of the worst years in recorded history) with projected occupancies edging toward 60 percent this year. Thus far, it has been concluded that a major new convention hotel is not economically feasible, even with generous public incentives.

PUBLIC AND PRIVATE CONTRIBUTIONS

These initiatives demonstrate the range of strategies available to the private sector to attract private hotel investment — as well as the pitfalls that can create obstacles. At their best, these partnerships make it possible to reduce hotel development costs, set the stage for more profitable hotel operations, and allow a government jurisdiction to safeguard public investment and achieve local economic development goals.

Generally, public contributions that can drive development of a hotel may include land at favorable lease terms, off-street parking facilities, construction/use rights of public space and marketing support. Hotel developers may also be granted the convention center's food and beverage service concession. This ancillary revenue can be an important step to offset the lower room rates often associated with delegate business. Among the contributions made by the hotel developer are equity funding, the track record of team members, a superior product development plan, and strong management and marketing.

In addition, the public and private entities must have controls in place to ensure that relationship objectives are maintained. A convention headquarters hotel, for example, must commit room nights to the convention center, even at the cost of displacing higher rated business. Conversely, the convention center must book events, which generate room nights, perhaps foregoing higher revenue-generating consumer shows that tend to be oriented to a local audience.

A range of successful private/public techniques are available to further these partnerships:

Site Control

Land values in urban or resort environments are generally very high with these costs typically representing a significant component of hotel development. Government participation is often essential, either by writing down the market value of a property or purchasing a property to lease to a hotel owner on a long-term basis at an economic cost.

Miami Beach's experience is instructive. The city in 1992 expanded its existing convention center located near City Hall, a location remote from Miami Beach's highly developed existing hotels. No new major hotels have been developed in 27 years. Studies commissioned by the city addressed several pivotal issues. It was determined that none of the existing hotels — clustered primarily at some distance along the coastline— would or could continuously sell room nights to major national conventions that desire to book the city's convention center. Additionally, major hotel developers would be unlikely to develop a new hotel away from the beach area without significant incentives. Arthur Andersen was asked to advise the city on incentive parameters required to entice developers and financial institutions in the development and financing of the 800-room hotel.

Among the most important of the incentives was site control.

Low-cost Financing

In the past five years, new full-service hotels have been extremely difficult to finance. Convention hotels, furthermore, are generally regarded as being of even higher risk — a result of the uncertainty related to occupancies and above-average development costs. As a result, public financing can be the key element in making a convention center hotel feasible.

Again, a number of options are available to the public sector. While tax- exempt public bond issues are subject to 'private purpose' limitations, there are techniques which can blend in public funding to privately owned and operated hotel ventures. These include financing and leasing back the 'public' areas of a hotel (or a parking, etc.) facility. Public revenues from hotel taxes or real property taxes may be designated for the facility through non-tax exempt issues. In addition, cities, counties and other government entities may offer certain operating guarantees, such as payment of debt service, for a specified period of time. Miami Beach, for example, agreed to issue $52 million in bonds as its share of land and construction of the $158 million convention hotel. The hotel developer — St. Moritz, a joint venture of Forest City and the Loews Corporation — will contribute $15 million in equity, with the balance financed with conventional debt.

In some cases cities have made equity investments in convention hotels. The municipality may become the junior equity partner in the hotel with 'first-in' risk capital, and 'last-out' return. In a broad policy sense, the city's rate of return is potentially greatly enhanced by an improved local economy, higher visitation and associated tax revenues.

Bond financing, and public ownership of the asset, for example, is a cornerstone of the financing structure for a new convention center hotel at McCormick Place, the final phase of its exposition center. The Metropolitan Pier and Exposition Authority, which controls McCormick Place, announced in March of this year that it plans to raise $110 million through a bond issue for the development of a new hotel adjacent to the center. The Authority will own the hotel, which is to have a minimum of 400 rooms and likely more. A third party will be selected to operate the property.

Other Public Incentives

Local governments also have incentive options that will have significant impact on the economies of building a convention headquarters hotel. These include incorporating public spaces and amenities, such as joint parking or meeting facilities to reduce the overall cost of the convention hotel. Municipalities may also provide property tax abatements, as well as redevelopment zone benefits such as expedited permitting and access to other public funding sources.

Structuring the Deal

From a development and operational standpoint, there are a number of challenges facing hotel companies as they consider convention headquarters hotels. In addition, many deals have failed because a city has insufficient resources to close a transaction, or lacks an understanding of the resources it can bring to bear in support of these developments. What is fundamentally at stake is shifting a portion of the risk from the developer to public entities, since the public jurisdiction stands to benefit economically if the hotel is a success.

More than a standard Request for Proposal (RFP) to attract a quality developer is often needed. The public sector must understand what types of incentives it has available to drive a project — and the best way to frame the RFP process. And it will clearly require specialized expertise to ensure that financial incentive structures make the most of available opportunities and that the expectations are realistic.

In setting parameters for competitive bidding on these projects, municipalities or other public jurisdictions need to be specific about certain factors, such as the hotel size, design, quality of facilities and amenities, and management. But rather than defining the competition in a rigid envelope, it is more important to ensure that respondents customize a proposal that meets the city's criteria and defined needs, and includes financial structures crafted to match the public resources available. Clearly defined procedures for evaluation of proposals are also crucial.

PUBLIC MARKET FINANCING

In a world where there is a general shortage of capital, hospitality companies must now work much harder in the global competition for money. And as the industry begins to recover in many countries from the excesses of the 1980s, the search is on for new solutions to the capital dilemma. Accentuating the dilemma is the fad that the losses of the early 1990s and the associated declines in property values have scared away many of the industry's traditional private capital providers. And they do not appear to be returning anytime soon. So it is not surprising that in some markets around the world there is strong interest in public financial markets as a place to seek capital, even though they tend to present some very unique challenges.

The international hotel industry has a long way to go in truly capitalizing on the opportunities afforded by public financial markets. The securitization of real estate has developed rapidly in recent years in US, but may be much longer in coming to other markets elsewhere, where traditional methods of financing are slow to change. Financial adversity will, however, force users of capital to source their needs in the public domain. It will require some big adjustments in approach and some serious corporate soul searching to get there. But it can be worth it and in a world of capital shortage, hospitality companies may have no choice but to force their way in.

For many years, the hotel industry benefited from the largesse of private institutional capital, primarily the insurance industry, savings institutions and commercial banks to fund property expansion and acquisition. With these resources no longer as available, the industry has been forced to turn to alternative sources such as the public market and has had to adjust to a new set of rules. As 1994 came to a close, Securitization of hotel property and mortgages in the United States was a very hot topic. Real Estate Investment Trusts or REITs (which distribute earnings from real estate, free of corporate taxes) had become high fliers in the stock market.

Having finally dealt with the structuring challenges that are unique to REITs and previously made hotel REIT formations problematic, a series of issues came to market in late 1993. These tended to be relatively small issues but they delivered some of the best stock performance in the REIT sector, with investor interest driven largely by the turnaround in the U.S. hotel industry that continues to this day. Following these initial successes, secondary offerings came to market during 1994 and the general enthusiasm was palpable. But with interest rate escalations throughout the year, the fervor began to fade and by late 1994, the market had retreated. Uncertainty concerning the outlook for hotel REITs was widespread with the conventional wisdom being that it would be a while before we would see any resurgence of interest.

There was a renewed interest in REITs late in 1995 signaled by the successful launch of the largest hotel REIT yet - the $305 million Patriot American issue involving a portfolio of 20 hotels. And earlier in the year, Starwood Capital successfully recapitalized Hotel Investors Trust, a "grandfathered" REIT that had been operating for years with a unique paired share structure that allows the REIT to manage as well as own property - something other REITs are not allowed to do. As these large hotel REITs have come to market, there appears to be an appreciation for size that translates into more favorable pricing. This suggests that small capitalization REITs may not see as much popularity as heretofore when they essentially had the market to themselves.

REITs both large and small are but examples, however, in a large public financial marketplace that is increasingly serving the capital needs of the U.S. hotel industry. During the last four years, approximately $4 billion of capital has been raised for publicly traded hotel companies and $1 billion for hotel REITs - split evenly between debt and equity. And the pace quickened in 1995 with a steadily rising stock market. Hotel industry financings were up by one-third over the prior year at approximately $2 billion.

Following the fall-off in the REIT market late in 1994, the market for new hotel REITs had been slow in returning. But with the success of the large Patriot American deal, the market seems ready for more. Interest rates, however, have a big impact on the REIT market, so future activity will be sensitive to interest rate volatility. on the basis of a stable interest environment, however, it is estimated that hotel REITs might represent as much as ~ billion in 19%. Easier to predict than volume is the style or structure of future hotel REIT financings. They are likely to be large and well-covered by Wall Street's research analysts - an essential element if an issue is to gain any respectability and following.

Hotel REITs have also tended to be all equity offerings with lines of credit to fund expansion - but these lines can run out quickly following an active property acquisition programme. Future hotel REITs will therefore need to develop capital structures that present blends of debt and equity in an effort to reduce the weighted cost of capital and provide for better balance as the capital base is expanded. Since quality sponsorship is so critical to success in public markets, it also appears likely that we will see fewer Initial Public Offerings and more secondary offerings involving the return to market of well-established hotel companies with a proven track record. No matter how much enthusiasm exists for the industry's positive economic situation, there is little doubt the focus in the future will be on management and its ability to deliver through the next cycle.

In addition to the return of hotel REITs last year, there was also a resurgence of activity involving "C" Corporations - traditionally structured companies that have historically been the main players in the public market, A series of new C-corp issues attracted a great deal of institutional investor interest, something that is not always as prevalent on the REIT side of the market. Some small C- corp issues also showed very strong growth stories as the hotel market has turned around. This has attracted a lot of new investors, which is clearly healthy in broadening the base of investor support for the industry.

An interesting trend is the growing acceptance of hotel real estate as part of a public company's balance sheet. Notwithstanding the tendency for the stock market to focus on short-term earnings, some of the recent hotel C corp issues have suggested that hotel property ownership can be appreciated, particularly if it delivers operating leverage in a period of rising occupancy. Of course this appreciation can disappear quickly in a downturn when the leverage works in reverse and delivers losses very quickly.

The public market tends to value a growth story. Working against this concept in the REIT arena is the requirement of the tax code that 95 percent of a REIT's earnings be distributed out to the investors each year. As a consequence, for those companies trying to build franchise value through customer relationships and in need of a constant source of reinvestment capital, the REIT structure is not generally a suitable vehicle. But for those with large real estate portfolios, judicious use of the REIT format for "off balance sheet" property financing can produce a satisfactory outcome. The lease format used by hotel REITs to address the tax laws' prohibition of involvement in the management of the property, tends to secure a long-term involvement with the property - something that is of particular value in a market where traditional property owner/manager relationships have become far more tenuous and unpredictable.

In the context of the hospitality industry at large, it is worth mentioning the gaming industry's involvement with public market financing. Gaming companies have long been involved with the public markets as a result of not being able to tap into private institutional sources of money. Without the respectability that it has today, gaming companies originally had to operate in the high-yield market. And as the gaming sector grew and the earnings escalated with new jurisdictions, a compelling story for gaming stocks has developed in recent years.

More recently we have seen the setbacks of poor press, some negative votes against new jurisdictions and one or two high-profile bankruptcies. This can quickly dampen the enthusiasm, and so it remains to be seen as to what the longer-term public market environment will be like for gaming companies. For those with experienced management, a well established franchise and customer following, and a position in established jurisdictions, there should be few difficulties. For those at the margin, however, it will be another story. And indeed we can expect to see a consolidation and shakeout as the gaming industry refocuses its attention on the strong players who are well-positioned to benefit from the trends in a variety of gaming jurisdictions across the country.

In evaluating whether to take a hospitality company to the public market for the first time, it is worth reviewing some simple fundamentals to determine if a company has what it takes to make it through the rigorous initial public offering process. Look for the following: the nature and energy level of the management team, stability of earnings, a solid outlook for growth and a focused story and business concept. Other issues to be contended with include the extent of existing leverage, the current owner's objectives and pricing expectations and the need for debt versus equity and their relative costs.

Otherwise successful companies also must recognize that taking a company public for the first time will probably mean facing a discount in value to account for the unknown. The countervailing view is that public market investors driven by the hype surrounding a bull market may value a high-profile hospitality company significantly in excess of what the private market might judge the stock to be worth - the herd mentality one might say. Timing is, of course, everything.

As Wall Street becomes more involved in hotel property financing, it is not surprising that the rating agencies have begun to play a role. Ratings have tended to be associated with the packaging of small hotel mortgages into Real Estate Mortgage Investment Conduits or "REMICs." Such conduits tranche the capital into various risk levels that carry a range of ratings and are priced accordingly. REMICs were expected to play a big role in hotel financing especially as these programmes were supported by some of the country's largest franchisors as a service to their franchisees. But they turned out to be relatively expensive for borrowers of small amounts. As the industry turned around, there was more competition from local banks willing to finally take a closer look at their neighborhood borrowers who had been ignored since the real estate collapse in 1991.

As the rating agencies look at hotel debt issues, the factors of importance include portfolio diversification (both geographic and by property type), the adequacy of management fees, the presence of satisfactory replacement reserves and the structure. Whether rating agencies can play a role in encouraging an expanded role for public market financing of the hotel sector remains to be seen. The early signs are that they are interested in understanding the business and appear willing to participate.

And yet even if there is a willingness on the part of the rating agency community to play a role, it must be recognized that at its heart, the public market is far more fickle than the private market. Sentiments of sup port and enthusiasm for an industry can evaporate quickly if there are unexpected setbacks. Conventional wisdom at the moment, however, seems to suggest that the U.S. hotel industry's fundamentals are positive and the upward trend in profitability should continue for at least two more years. Demand for hotel rooms, however, tracks extremely closely with the underlying change in Gross Domestic Product. So as goes the economy, thus will follow the hotel industry. And if the economy falters, expect to see some major interruption in the otherwise rosy outlook for hotel stocks and debt issues. But even if the industry continues on its present positive track, we should not assume that the public markets will provide all of the answers to the liquidity crisis for the industry.

Because of the hotel industry's fragmented structure, its real estate orientation and its general reputation as part real estate/part business, we have not seen as many publicly quoted hotel companies as one might expect in an industry of its size. This hopefully will change in future years as the hospitality industry gains further respectability and hotel corporations enlarged through the process of consolidation seek broader access to public capital.

Consolidation can also have a counterpoint, however, and in the U.S. hotel and gaming industries this means de-consolidation. Two companies are of particular note in having split or attempted to split their gaming and hotel operations - Promus and Hilton. Marriott Corporation split for different reasons in an attempt to separate their real estate from their operational activities. And finally Sheraton Hotels, a stalwart of the U.S. hospitality scene, is now part of a split-up by parent ITT of its varied businesses into three groupings. The first, ITT Destinations, is the consolidation of its hospitality, gaming, sports and entertainment businesses. The public market reactions to these reconstitutions of hospitality companies have by-and-large been favorable, suggesting that it pays to continuously look "outside the organizational box" when trying to create shareholder value.

As hotel groups become larger and operate on a truly global basis, we are likely to see simultaneous hotel company listings in key financial markets around the world such as New York, London and Tokyo. one of the advantages of such international public market exposure relates to the quest that many hospitality companies have for global brand presence. Customer focus deriving from a brand strategy can quite reasonably tie into shareholder relationships on a global scale. It is just a matter of time.

World Finance Markets

In the past, many lenders and institutional and individual investors have viewed the hospitality industry somewhat suspiciously, and have preferred to provide corporate debt to hotel companies or to purchase shares in quoted hotel companies to spread sector risk as widely as possible. This preference has meant that the industry has been characterized by relatively unsophisticated financings.

The ownership structure of the industry in the United Kingdom has also been of influence in this regard. Hotels tend to be owner-operated and, with relatively few exceptions, the major hotel owning and operating companies are subsidiaries of conglomerates. Where capital has been required for development and M&A activity at such companies, it has normally been provided by the parent company since, generally speaking, corporate debt at such a level is rather less expensive than project or deal-specific debt.

In the United Kingdom there are relatively few independent hotel management companies operating hotels under franchises from the major international brands. In the United States such independent companies have been great users of public market capital. Those which do exist in the United Kingdom are small - in most instances operating two or three hotels. Development and acquisitions activity at such companies tend to be financed on a project-by-project basis with security provided by the asset to be financed plus, in many cases, additional company or personal guarantees. The one major exception to this general rule is the Whitbread Hotel Group (formerly Scott's Hotels), which owns and operates 13 hotels under franchise agreements with Marriott International. Whitbread Hotels Group, however, is a relatively small subsidiary of Whitbread PLC the brewing company, and funds for the £185 million acquisition of the 13 Scott's hotels were provided by the parent company.

Special share issues (such as rights issues and convertible preference share issues), however, have been used among the relatively few quoted "pure" hotel companies - particularly during the late 1980s. Oueen's Moat Houses financed a series of corporate and individual hotel property acquisitions via rights issues.

Turning to the future in the United Kingdom, given the capital intensive nature of the industry, we have observed an increasing interest among both the major conglomerates and the (few) independent hotel owned management companies in innovative financing methods - particularly in off-balance sheet financing. We believe that this interest will extend in the future to public capital markets.

With the Japanese economy struggling for a soft landing and with banks still trying to deal with the challenges posed by their sizable exposure to real estate, the hospitality industry does not maintain any particular visibility in the public markets. The hospitality sector has been traditionally housed in large corporations with financing obscured from public view.

And in Germany, the hospitality industry's experience with the public markets is in its developmental stages, reports Hospitality Consulting Director John Litzenberger of Arthur Andersen's Frankfurt office. Kempinski is the only publicly quoted company with just six hotels in Germany and a total portfolio of only 30 properties. With an overbuilt domestic market, there is little demand for new capital, public or otherwise to fund new activities. The large German chains are by-and-large privately owned — Maritim, Steigenberger and Arabella — and do not come to the public market for capital. Closed-end property funds that do trade publicly will have some exposure to hotel real estate but it tends to be mixed into a large diversified portfolio. In summary, the German hospitality sector clearly is a long way from using public market financing in the way that companies do in the United States. This might change in the future, suggests Litzenberger, but it will be a long rime in the making.

In Australia, Phil Kasselis, Director of Hospitality Consulting in the firm's Sydney office, reports that the Australian Stock Exchange has 16 listed companies in a Tourism and Leisure Index. The TL Index was established in 1994 with over half the index made up of casino stocks. The index outperformed the market by a factor of 3:1 in 1995, confirming the enthusiasm investors have for the fast developing gaming industry and the fundamentals of the hotel sector, where demand growth continues to outstrip supply and should continue to do so for the next several years and probably up to the year 2000 when Sydney hosts the Olympics.

In the Australian property funds, where hotels as an asset class are generally under-represented, we should see an increase in the allocation of capital to this sector as profits return and the hotel industry outlook remains positive. Casino operators, hotel owners and hotel management companies will also expand their presence in the public financial markets, finding it a cheaper and easier way to raise capital than traditional bank debt. Large institutions are also likely to increase their involvement with publicly listed hospitality companies.

BUDGETING IN HOSPITALITY INDUSTRY

Today's hotel companies are more competitive and dynamic than ever before. As a result, the days when hotel budgeting was merely a routine process of incrementally increasing the prior year revenues and expenses have long ended. Successful hospitality companies are constantly seeking ways to improve their ability to predict future operations and related resource requirements, enabling them to adjust their budget plans as needed to stay ahead of the competition. Not only does this alter the importance of the budget and forecast process; but, it also changes the traditional methods used of incremental, fixed and flexible budgeting processes.

The hospitality industry's traditional method of budgeting revenues and expenses has been the same for decades. Up to now, the most commonly used methods have been Incremental Budgeting and Fixed or Flexible Budgeting.

— *Incremental Budgeting*: this method is widely used in the hospitality industry and generally entails budgeting revenues and expenses based on the prior period adjusting for inflation by a percentage.

— *Fixed and Flexible Budgeting* is usually for one specific expense item that is referred to as 'fixed'. A budget adjusted for a change in the level of activity is called a 'flexed' or 'flexible' budget, which means that when the level of activity changes, it is expected that the total of all costs will change. Information about how each type of cost behaves is related to how income enables budgets to be adjusted for different levels of activity. If actual results are to be compared with budgets for the purposes of performance measurement - for example, cost per occupied room, percentage of expenses, etc. - such adjustments would be necessary to ensure the comparison is reasonable.

Hotels most often budget simply by increasing the Key Performance Indicators (KPI) by a targeted percentage or by a given CPI index on a monthly basis, and then calling it a day without any of the necessary detailed explanations to support these expenses. Such budgeting and forecasting methods have created a tremendous short fall in future projections that put owners in a difficult situation when confronted by investors and lenders.

Over the past few years, however, tremendous technological improvements have been made to enhance revenue budgeting tools. There are now a few revenue yield management systems available to improve ADR, market penetration and RevPar. This has helped many hospitality companies improve market share, penetration and hotel positioning in each market. So it would also seem that with all the new technology available it should be easy for hoteliers to use the more informative Zero Base Budgeting method.

Zero Base Budgeting

Zero based budgeting derives from the idea that such budgets are developed from a zero base; that is) at the beginning of the budget process, all budget accounts have a value of ZERO. This is in sharp contrast to the incremental budgeting system where generally a new budget tends to start with a balance at least equal to last year's total balance, or an estimate of it.

The goal of preparing a zero base budget is to achieve an optimal allocation of resources that incremental and other budgeting methods are less likely to present. Zero Based Budgeting starts by asking managers to identify and justify their area(s) of work in terms of business volumes.

Zero Based Budgeting forces managers to justify their work by saying to them that unless and until they put forward a budget that more senior management can support, at least to a large extent; then the budget will not be approved. If Zero Based Budgeting is applied as literally as it is designed, then unjustified work and expenses would simply stop.

An effective zero base budgeting system benefits organizations in several ways. It will:

— Focus the budget process on a comprehensive analysis of objectives and needs

— Combine planning and budgeting into a single process

— Cause managers to evaluate in detail the cost effectiveness of their operations

— Expand management participation in planning and budgeting at all levels of the organization

Zero Based Budgeting process has a lot to offer it in terms of the way it forces management at all levels of an organization to become involved in the budgeting process. Zero Based Budgeting is built on the concept that what one expects in the future will be dependant on the ability to persuade the rest of the management team that it is deserved.

Advantages of Zero-Based Budgeting

1. Results in efficient allocation of resources as it is based on needs and benefits.

2. Drives managers to find out cost effective ways to improve operations.

3. Detects inflated budgets.

4. Useful for service department where the output is difficult to identify.

5. Increases staff motivation by providing greater initiative and responsibility in decision-making.

6. Increases communication and coordination within the organization.

7. Identifies and eliminates wastage and obsolete operations.

Disadvantages of Zero-Based Budgeting

1. Forced to justify every detail related to expenditure.

2.   Difficult to implement using spreadsheets (would require a database application to be most effective).

3.   It is very time-consuming if justification sheets are done using spreadsheets.

4.   Necessary to train managers on the concept. Zero Based Budgeting should be clearly understood by managers at various levels otherwise it cannot be successfully implemented.

5.   Difficult to administer and communicate the budgeting process because more managers are involved in the process.

Hotel owners are looking for detailed justification of how each dollar is spent and how well their asset is managed. The understanding of expenses and their relationship to the revenues, room nights, food covers and other business indicators that affect profitability is critical, and the lack of documentation explaining this relationship can make the process a very tedious one. A good budget package should eliminate the old fashion spreadsheet budgets and give operators the flexibility to create different scenarios and associate each expense as it relates to the business. This is necessary because in the hospitality industry, expenses are constantly increasing while the revenue streams are highly variable. Database budgets will not only facilitate the preparation of zero based budgets and forecasts, but also will assist operators with providing sufficient detailed information for the hotel owners and asset managers when reviewing the annual budgets and the monthly forecasts.

It is time for hotel companies and individual hotel operators to break the paradigm of budgeting by spreadsheets and seek for the technological help to get up to speed with the tools that will help provide accurate information.Budgeting by spreadsheets is the way of the past and inaccuracy is the most likely outcome.

A budget/forecast with sufficient supporting documentation will be most likely approved faster. The variances to actual would be then easier to explain and easier to manage than a budget prepared by simple marginal increases over prior years. It is time to make department managers part of the planning process and accountable for their budgets and forecast instead of the usual process where hotel controllers are expected to the do all of this alone.

3

Food Cost Control

Food cost represents the largest controllable cost center for the hotelier yet historically hotels have been challenged by how best to manage this entity. Key to achieving the last few points in hotel profitability is the ability to manage food inventory within the hotel. The challenge is these systems are traditionally very complex to maintain and are difficult to execute at the store level.

FOOD AND BEVERAGE REVENUES

There are many reasons why hotel food and Beverage profits are not what we would like them to be. Foremost among them is usually the fact that revenues are not as high as they might be. The lack of separate identity and entrances for outlets has a negative impact but for the most part hoteliers aren't the street fighting promoters our free standing restaurant counterparts are. There are some subtle differences that make a lot of sense. Think about how you'd spend your finite promotional dollars if you had a choice between promoting the hotel in its entirety or just a profitable restaurant outlet. Clearly it makes more sense to advertise the hotel and its services or to have the sales staff either build commercial room demand or pursue group room bookings. These items have profit margins in excess of 75 - 80%.

A hotel's Food and Beverage department is an exception if profit exceeds 20%. In both cases as hoteliers must admit, administrative, marketing, maintenance and utilities expenses are not deductions from these margins. Unlike the restaurant counterparts who must bear all these expenses directly we shuffle them off as Unallocated Expenses. In the end it makes sense because most hotel Food and Beverage revenues are driven by the Rooms Department's level of activity and the buildings and operational structures are not such that some expenses can be isolated cost effectively.

Can you imagine the time required to allocate the credit card commission expenses for Food and Beverage charged to the guest rooms from those having to do with the Telephone Department and room sales? So what do we think the answer is to Food and Beverage profitability in a hotel environment? Increase hotel guest usage, increase hotel guest average checks, and increase outside patronage from the community. You say those things are obvious but do you have a mini-business plan for each of your Food and Beverage outlets? Does it address those items? Is it funded, are all the departments' employees involved and excited about it? Are the key players motivated with incentives to make the plans succeed? Mini-business plan? You know, like the one you have for the hotel; revenue and expense goals in detail, staffing plan, capital budget, menu plan and outlet market plan. These are not all new things, everything but the menu plan and outlet market plan should be in your hotel's annual business plan, so preparing a mini-plan for each Food and Beverage outlet should not be a monumental task.

We refer to these plans as mini-plans because they can be three small lists: standard hotel procedures, one time promotions and advertising. Standard hotel procedures are simple things like having the reception staff mention the outlets to registering guests and having the bell staff mention that night's restaurant specials while the guest is a captive audience.

Standard hotel procedures must include services, attitudes and amenities that are very appealing to the hotel's guests. Services are kind of obvious but attitudes are a little tougher. Rather than exclusively hiring experienced servers look for people with a positive, cheerful outgoing attitude that either have experience or are trainable. A cheerful good attitude will over-come a lot of service and even quality problems, assuming they are short term! Your servers must enjoy their patrons, thank them for coming, ask them if they will be in tomorrow, how their room is, etc. In short they must care. It will help the food and Beverage outlets and the hotel in general.

Amenities are a more exciting and creative issue. Sure there should be an assortment of newspapers at breakfast and with room service. But what about a heated pot of coffee so that the patrons don't have to wait to be bothered by, "...more coffee?" every few minutes. Can you promote your restaurant or coffee shop as the area's power breakfast meeting place? Offer cut fruit with every order for the health conscious and thick slab bacon or what ever is locally popular for the heavy eaters. Why not free shoe shines as patrons leave and for people waiting for a table or for joiners? Dare to be different and work hard to find out what your hotel guests and surrounding community want. Who eats at Perkins and Bakers Square and why? What is so good and unique about them that can't be copied?

Advertising for food and beverage outlets ranges from the basics like the Yellow Pages and entertainment directories to such media as radio and television. Any media that can be obtained for free is good as long as one has some control over it. Trade outs are always a good idea. The best trade a Food and Beverage manager can arrange is rooms for advertising! Next to that, beverage for advertising is good if it can be obtained on some multiple like four advertising dollars for one beverage dollar. Doing joint promotions with media outlets is especially effective if one can obtain extra advertising unrelated to the promotion at a later time in order to stay in the audience's mind. Never forget the power of good press releases. These should be done for all conventions, banquets, menu changes, new entertainment, etc. Invite the press in to try new menus and to witness promotions. Charities are good tie ins.

BRANDING OF FOOD AND BEVERAGE

Hotel guests generally enjoy the convenience of F&B outlets, hut when given the chance, they frequently choose a known brand off the premises, leaving a hotel for nearby restaurant chains. In the process, they take much-desired dining dollars with them. As customers become more brand—aware, competition for F&B business continues to grow in importance for many hotels.

From the hotel's perspective, a joint venture or outsourcing arrangement can provide a combination of restaurant skills and brand strength, often supported by national advertising. Hotels adding branded restaurants have reported improved F&B volume, including room service sales, as well as an attendant increase in occupancy and average rate. In a period of hospitality industry consolidation, branded restaurants may become a point of differentiation among hotel properties. Restaurant companies, of course, also stand to gain from this flurry of alliances. In today's market, many companies are being forced to look outside traditional development options and to consider new types of locations.

Competencies and Outsourcing

During the early 1990s, businesses faced the difficult task of assessing procedural strengths and weaknesses to trim fat and streamline processes. Outsourcing non-critical activities allowed companies to extend their organisational core competencies. The hospitality and leisure industry was no exception to this trend. During the past few years, hotels have been called on to assess their core competencies, while attempting to shed responsibility for non-core activities.

Core competencies can be defined as those unique disciplines that confer competitive advantage, motivating customers to buy a company's goods and services over those of a competitor. As this decade comes to a close, businesses are further dividing the non-core segment into two categories:

1. essential non-core and
2. non-essential non-core.

Those activities that are both non-core and non-essential are being shut down. Processes that are essential, but "non-core," become prime candidates for outsourcing. Providing quality rooms and guest services remains a hotel's primary function. The F&B function, however, commands attention because of its importance to guest satisfaction and brand management. Many hoteliers, however, make the mistake of thinking that it takes the same competencies to operate a restaurant as it does to run a hotel. In actual fact, the restaurant business requires a different set of skills, including more attention to detail, than rooms management. By reengineering F&B operations, hotel management has the opportunity to redirect energies from the restaurant business and focus efforts on enhancing hotel operations and profitability and, potentially, shareholder value.

Outsourcing Partnerships

Outsourcing partnerships typically bring together organisations with diverse capabilities. Understanding what each side of the equation requires to succeed is essential. This important guideline applies whether a hotel owner is considering outsourcing all or part of its F&B operations to a restaurant chain, or merely outsourcing its coffee shop to a local restaurateur.

Historically, restaurant chains have been strict about the demographics and economic indicators in a market before committing to a location. And until recently, there was no shortage of suitable sites. Prime demographic indicators include a mix of office space, upper-middle class residences, and upscale apartments with higher-income professionals looking for an element of fun. If a potential restaurant site was not viewed as a "home run" location, a restaurateur would typically pass on a development opportunity. Due to increased competition and a limited number of prime sites, restaurant companies have found they must go further afield than in the past, breaking traditional biases about what locations work.

Until recently, hotels have been reluctant to outsource their F&B operations - or single restaurants. Traditionally, hotel management viewed F&B operations as a low margin or unprofitable service required to enhance guest satisfaction. As such, F&B profitability was always examined with a mentality of "minimizing a loss." As a way to rationalise an unprofitable track record, hotel management often convinced itself that there was insufficient demand for profitable F&B operations.

In addition, as hotels emerged from the last recession and downturn in hotel profitability, emphasis was placed on the renovation of guestrooms, lobbies and banquet space over F&B outlets. Based on historical trends, renovation priority has consistently been given to profit-generating guestrooms over unprofitable food and beverage operations.

Additionally, hotels opting to create a new concept or introduce an existing, branded concept may find start-up costs to he exorbitant. Estimated costs of upgrading a food and beverage outlet to a chain's specified standards range from $500,000 to $1.5 million, depending on the extent of renovation and equipment purchases required. Of course, outsourcing operations to a local restaurateur would likely cost far less.

The hotel, however, would not benefit from the brand recognition associated with a larger, more established name in the marketplace. Lastly, hotel management companies earning fees based on gross revenue may be reluctant to reduce the base on which their management fee is calculated. This may prompt hotel owners and managers to reassess their management position. Frequently the parties agree to either renegotiate revenue-based fee percentages or include revenues earned by third-party F&B operators in the management fee calculations.

Despite the issues associated with outsourcing of food and beverage operations, there are compelling reasons for hotels to consider this option. Brand strength and competitive positioning for the hotel property are among the most important.

Branding and Repositioning

Why is it that guests often prefer to patronise known brands rather than a hotel's stand-alone F&B outlet? While consumers are more brand aware than ever before, research suggests there may even be a perceived stigma associated with dining in a hotel restaurant. Integrating a branded concept into a hotel is a way to minimize the stigma, bringing guests back to the hotel outlets and reducing internal costs. Additionally, familiar dining concepts seem to put travelers at ease. Customers who are away from home and out of their element are comforted by the availability and consistency that accompanies a known brand name product.

In 1995 Choice Hotels surveyed its full service hotels and learned that most of its properties experienced a great deal of difficulty keeping restaurants profitable. Reported food expenditures of 40 to 50 percent of their F&B revenues, accompanied by labour costs of 45 to 50 percent, made it virtually impossible to generate a profit, according to Barbara Shuster, Director of Choice Hotels International's Choice Picks programme. To combat this trend, select Choice hotels implemented a food court concept in the F&B area, and were surprised to see food and labour costs on F&B revenues drop to an average of 32 percent and 28 percent, respectively. In addition to brand identity, most operators find that guests are not only more willing to patronise high-street brands conveniently situated within the hotel, but they are also willing to pay more for the privilege of dining with a familiar concept. Increased willingness to dine coupled with increased willingness to spend results in increased revenues.

Hotels introducing a branded restaurant into their property often experience higher external traffic. Market exposure translates into increased outlet revenue and enhanced customer perception of the F&B outlet brand name, as well as enhanced customer perception of the hotel itself. Thus the net result of rebranding and repositioning can be increased profit and enhanced shareholder value.

Before taking the plunge into the world of outsourced or reengineered F&B operations, hotel management must take several factors into consideration:

Competition

No outsourcing arrangement will work, unless there is market demand. Competitive analysis should include restaurants in neighboring hotels, as well as stand-alone restaurants in the area. Profitability issues and pricing a new outlet also must be considered in the market context. Many hotels find that the brand name restaurant buys recognition in the customer 5 mind and creates a draw for business. The partnered restaurant sets the hotel apart from other hotels in the area and segment by providing a strong competitive and marketing advantage.

Marketing

The hotelier and restaurateur must establish responsibility for marketing of the new concept. Frequently hotels agree to advertise the operator in the guestrooms, although the outlet typically absorbs the cost of signage in the rooms and throughout the hotel. Additionally, the restaurateur typically assumes responsibility and accountability for all external advertising.

Guest expectations

The goal of outsourcing F&B operations is to enhance profitability by increasing internal as well as external traffic, without losing the current customer base. It is essential to consider guest reaction to the change in F&B concept. If a negative reaction is anticipated, a hotelier risks losing its customer base and thus future earning potential to the competition.

Management styles

It is important to look at both the local and corporate management styles of both the hotelier and restaurateur, Incompatibility of the two styles could result in a rocky relationship and tumultuous times. In order to avoid this friction, some hotels have found it advantageous to appoint the general manager of the restaurant to the hotel's executive team, thereby creating a sense of responsibility and belonging and enhancing relationships throughout the organisation.

Terms of the Contract

The operational terms of the contract must be set out in detail. Quality standards and monitoring mechanisms should be detailed to ensure that the restaurant is operated at a standard that is acceptable and complementary to that of the hotel. Additionally, hours of restaurant operation, including room service, are critical specifications. As breakfast is typically a money -

generating activity, and frequently not one that restaurant chain operators are accustomed to serving, many hoteliers prefer to maintain responsibility for this meal. However, concessions affecting profitability occasionally need to be made in order to solidify a working relationship.

A successful outsourcing relationship involves first and foremost trust and cohesion between the two partners. Of course, operational terms must be clearly detailed and make economic sense for both parties. While the requirements of a restaurant chain may be more stringent and costly than those of an independent restaurant operator, the basic tenets of a trusting partnership, complementary levels of quality, compatible clientele and a location with sufficient demand to justify a restaurant operation are all necessary. Successful implementation of an F&B outsourcing partnership can result in enhanced brand recognition and profitability for both the hotelier and the restaurateur.

Structuring an Outsourcing Partnership

Leasing

A hotel leases a room or section of the hotel, preferably with self-contained back-of-the-house areas in exchange for a flat fee and/or a percentage of sales. Statistics are not available for this type of transaction, as leasing deals vary depending on the area of space being leased, the brand being introduced into the market, the location of the hotel and agreements that may have been established by a head office. The hotel benefits by receiving a guaranteed rent, plus a revenue "top-up" each month. The landlord, however, loses control of F&B operations. Management must agree to let someone else run the show.

Franchising

This option suits a hotel seeking to change a restaurant concept without investing in an internal and potentially untested concept. The hotel buys an established brand and system for a fee. The process begins with an upfront payment - a buy-in to the right to operate a better known and more profitable concept. Frequently, the franchisor requires the hotel to make an additional payment for a capital investment, requiring a purchase of specified equipment. Under the franchising terms, the hotel pays the franchisor a royalty fee, usually based on a percentage of sales, for the privilege of using the name and resources.

Throughout the relationship, it is the franchisees responsibility to ensure that hotel staff is adequately trained to assure quality consistent with other branded sites. Marriott International was one of the first major hotel chains to enter into F&B franchising arrangements, with a 1989 franchising partnership with Pizza Hut. Marriott has since introduced Pizza Hut outlets and in-room dining options at many of its properties throughout the world.

Joint Venture

This is a variant of franchising and contracting. The hotelier creates a strategic alliance with a known, successful restaurateur. The two parties create a separate financial company, which is appointed as the lessee of the restaurant. The new organisation, the restaurant lessee., then outsources the F&B operations to the restaurateur. Typically the hotel provides the capital expenditures and the restaurateur brings intellectual property and expertise. The two parties share the successes and the related profits.

For example, Marco Pierre White formed a joint venture with Granada hotels valued at £2 million to provide F&B services at seven select Forte hotels in the UK. The new organisation, MPW Criterion, will reengineer the way select Granada hotel F&B outlets do business. Additionally, before its merger with Starwood Lodging, ITT Corporation, owner of Sheraton Hotels and Caesar's Casinos, formed a partnership with Planet Hollywood International to develop, construct and manage Planet Hollywood - themed casinos in Las Vegas and Atlantic City. The two parties were also entertaining the idea of converting existing hotel outlets into Planet Hollywood restaurants.

Proprietary Brands

Hotel chains can create a proprietary brand, introducing the concept into all of its properties. This approach appeals to guests who enjoy consistency throughout a hotel chain. However, it is difficult to gain wider customer identity outside of the hotel properties. Marriott, for example, already has its own concepts in place, including JW's Steakhouse, Allie's American Grille and Champion's Bar. Likewise, Regal Hotels is growing its own brands, including Hard Edged and Morrisey's Pub, in several of its hotels as well as developing F&B solutions through its alliance with The Restaurant Partnership.

STEPS TO CONTROL FOOD COST

Following are some essential steps to control food cost.

1. *Ordering* - The first step is to order right. Having detailed recipes, designing purchasing specifications, doing comparative shopping based on those

specifications, and comparing quality, price and service, etc. Oh yes, don't order too early in order to avoid spoilage, wasted storage space and lost interest on your money. Don't order too late, so premium costs and delivery charges accrue.

2. *Receiving* - The fundamentals are obvious: count; weigh; inspect for condition and quality; verify against the purchase order; keep the receiving area clean and uncluttered; limit access to the receiving area; train the person receiving and make him or her responsible. Get credit memos from the delivery driver.

3. *Storing* - Is the method and place of storage for the various items appropriate for the item? Is it secure from pilferage? Are the shelves strong enough for the product, allow air circulation and easy to clean? Are all items stored at a temperature appropriate for that product? Are items dated (with year, in some cases) and priced? Is the storage area orderly and clean? Should shelves be labeled and maybe even stocking quantities noted?

4. *Issuing* - What is issuing based on? Who has access and or authority to issue or take things from the secured store rooms and walk-ins? Are issues being made in appropriate quantities and at appropriate times? Is there a relationship to volume or reasonable par stocks? Are issues being accounted for? Is a perpetual inventory or sign out sheet designed specifically for your operation or a particular store room in use?

5. *Preparation* - Phrases that come to mind include: trim properly; use trimmings for stock pots and other recipes. Proper tools, sharp knives, clean and neat working area, enforcing a policy of following recipes, and having photos of finished products available and used regularly are also critical.

6. *Cooking* - Various considerations here. Proper temperatures, proper cooking times, following recipes carefully, using photographs of finished products, correct size, material, and type of utensils and cookware, clean work area.

7. *Serving* - Serving is not only about portion control, it is also about decisions made regarding portion size and presentation. With a buffet, it is obvious. Proper serving utensils, proper holding/serving equipment, right presentation order, plate sizes, etc. In a bar its easy, too. Jiggers or other measuring and control devices and very strict discipline. The discipline isn't easy especially in tight labor markets. Dining room service should be easy to control using good kitchen supervisors, trained cooks, photographs for both cooks and servers, etc. Watch what comes back from bused tables to see if portions are proper. Marketing decisions may drive large portions but if the patrons are not eating it or taking it home, the portion size or the recipe should be reconsidered. Proper china for each item served is important for both presentation and portion control.

Work hard on your cost controls and be consistent about them. One element of controlling food cost covers all seven categories: thorough training. Give your staff the ability and knowledge and confidence to do their jobs properly and to your specifications. Inconsistency and failure to enforce procedures will drive costs skyward. Failure here is like throwing money away.

4

Hotel Investment Management

During the past several years the hotel industry has grown from being one of the worst to one of the top performing investment asset classes. And during this same time the strong investment performance of hotels has attracted substantial investment capital. More recently returns (on hotel investments) have leveled off for most hotels and have actually declined for many types of hotel investments. And as a result the industry is already experiencing the contraction of investment capital.

The on-going availability of investment capital can be expected to ultimately be closely linked to investment return performance (in particular relative to the risk and returns of alternative investments). And accordingly, one of the major challenges of the industry going forward will be maintaining hotel investment returns at levels adequate to continue to attract investment capital.

The information available on investment performance for the hospitality industry historically has been very limited. For several years the industry has tracked the numerator (or overall "profit" or cash flow generated by hotels) but has been unable to relate this number to a denominator (or the total dollars invested in hotels) at a given point in time. Also in the past the industry has not been able to isolate the capital appreciation versus income return components for hotels nor to develop a total investment return performance barometer/indices for the industry.

In response to the need for better industry investment return performance data, the American Hotel & Motel Association's Industry Real Estate Financial Advisory Council, in conjunction with Cornell University, developed the "Lodging Property Index". The index, initially published in 1996, represents the first of its kind in the hotel industry. While the index represents a great leap forward in the compilation of return on investment performance numbers for hotels, the information available for the industry as a whole is still very limited. Going forward the industry will need to focus on expanding the return on investment performance data available for the industry as a whole to provide a more reliable barometer for investors to evaluate hotel investment performance.

With the tremendous emphasis in recent years on the deal making or transaction side of the business as an industry we have lost focus on the customer, the employee and the underlying business fundamentals of operating hotels.

The customer - recent surveys indicate that hotel customer satisfaction is at an all time low (i.e. since first being tracked in the early 90's).

The employee - employee turnover for the industry as a whole is also at an all time high.

Underlying Business Fundamentals - there continue to be substantial opportunities for many hotels to improve both revenue and expense performance. For many hotels there are untapped revenue and yield management opportunities. And on the expense side, promotion and distribution costs and labor management represent areas for further improving performance. Going forward we can anticipate a return to the basics — a renewed focus on the customer, the employee and the management of revenue and expenses.

FINANCIAL PERFORMANCE MONITORING

With advances in technology, there is a tremendous amount of information (financial and sales and marketing in particular) available for review and analysis. On the one hand the voluminous information available can be very helpful for better understanding and diagnosing problems as well as for identifying areas for improving performance. Unfortunately, on the other, the amount of information potentially available to be reviewed and analyzed can be very overwhelming.

One of the major challenges in the future will be to streamline reporting to both facilitate comprehension as well as to potentially bridge the tremendous communication gaps (between investor and operational reporting; between asset and property managers; between corporate and on-site management and even among executive committee members) emerging.

SHAREHOLDER/INVESTOR REPORTING

The information in many shareholder and investor reports, for REIT's in particular, is currently presented at a very high level of aggregation making it very difficult and in some instances virtually impossible to really understand what is going on an individual property basis. Additionally, in some instances critical information (i.e. on revenue statistics and margin performance) even at the portfolio level, let alone at the individual property level, has been missing in public offering and/or shareholder reports.

With declines in return on investment performance, we can anticipate that owners and investors will increasingly want better information to evaluate performance. And in particular, we can expect that investors will want better information on both the fundamentals underlying performance overall (i.e. margin performance) as well as look for more detail to be provided on the performance of the individual assets (hotels) in a portfolio, to better understand how the performance of an individual hotel is contributing to the performance of the portfolio as a whole.

TECHNOLOGY

There are several technology issues that can be expected to represent on-going challenges for hotel owners/asset managers in the future. First is the basic challenge of staying informed! Technology currently represents one of the largest capital investment areas. To make informed decisions (in committing potentially very substantial investment dollars) it is critical that owners/asset managers understand a hotels basic (or from a managerial perspective) technology needs and the cost versus benefits of alternative approaches to addressing them.

We can anticipate that the issues of the ownership of data along with other proprietary as well as interface issues will continue to evolve as potential major areas of concern. And increasingly we are seeing challenges particularly in the area of yield management in bridging the automated versus cognitive or learning application perspectives in technology.

ALIGNMENT OF INTERESTS

While historically conflicts of interest have focused primarily on third party management and/or franchise issues, more recently we have seen conflicts of interest develop in other areas. With the significant changes in the forms of ownership of hotels experienced in the past few years, we are seeing potential conflicts emerge in certain investment structures.

Additionally, with advances in technology along with the significant increase in merger and acquisitions activity in recent years, new areas of potential conflicts have also emerged that will need to be addressed in the future. In the area of technology, the issues of proprietary systems and the ownership of data can be expected to present challenges and possible conflicts between an owner/ investor and a third party chain and/or franchisor's interests. And with the substantial recent merger and acquisitions activity, potential conflicts of interest are emerging—in the sales and marketing area in particular.

MANAGEMENT CONTRACTS

Going forward we can anticipate that owners/investors will place much greater emphasis on managing third party operator/manager risk and exposure issues. Delegations of authority and control, indemnifications, default and termination provisions etc. will be expanded and further defined to provide for better alignment of operator accountability with delegations of authority and control and to better address potential conflicts of interest.

We can also anticipate that greater focus will be placed on managing transition and exit strategy issues and concerns. Quite simply, if a major problem and/or conflict of interest develops an owner needs the ability to timely resolve it—or if it cannot be resolved (which is potentially the case with certain inherent conflicts of interest that are emerging) the ability to reasonably terminate the contract.

And as part of better managing transition exposure in the future, the issues of the ownership of books and records, proprietary computer systems, interim reservations system support, employee rights obligations and responsibilities, the handling of business on the books, the managing of public relations exposure etc.—all need to be addressed up front to mitigate what can be tremendous exposure for a hotel owner if for whatever reason a change in management is necessary.

FRANCHISE CONTRACT RELATIONSHIPS

Shorter term contracts, improved alignment of interests (of franchisor and franchisee), greater focus on direct sales (versus mass advertising and promotion strategies), more potential ala carte value added offerings versus mandatory programme requirements—are all areas that we can anticipate the industry will focus on in the future. Additionally, the internet—and the marketing and distribution alternatives it can provide— can be expected to potentially greatly level the playing field between franchisors and franchisees for certain types of hotels.

CAPITAL ASSET PRESERVATION

Historically, the hotel industry has lagged far behind other industries in managing the physical assets underlying a hotel investment. There is tremendous untapped potential to improve hotel investment performance via mitigating capital reinvestment exposure through improved preventative maintenance programmes and improved capital investment decision making. Going forward we can anticipate that much greater emphasis will be placed both on better preserving capital assets as well as improving up front decision making when initially purchasing capital items.

HUMAN RESOURCES

With the tremendous focus in recent years on the transaction side of the business, the industry has lost substantial focus on one of the most critical components of a hotel investment...namely the employee. The hotel business is first and foremost a people business. Neither the most glamorous of hotels nor the most sophisticated or creative financial transactions can insure success in the hotel industry. But rather it is consistently the employees—well trained and motivated employees—that ultimately make the difference in a hotel investment.

Human resource management issues—from recruiting, training and motivating employees to managing turnover and labor costs—can be expected to represent huge challenges in the future. Going forward addressing these same issues is not only the right thing to do but represents one of, if not the single greatest opportunity, for improving investment performance.

INVESTING IN TECHNOLOGY FOR COMPETITIVE ADVANTAGE

Today's hospitality industry technology represents a legacy reflecting the computer industry's capabilities during the last two decades and the willingness of hotel executives to embrace its products. We stand the latest wave of a historical evolution beginning with the early hotel accounting systems in the 1960s and early 1970s.

These were followed by a variety of front office systems introduced in the 1980s and finally to today's property management systems and the latest efforts in integrated customer information systems, data warehouses and the like.But, in recent years, critics have been increasingly harsh with their comments on the computer systems and software applications used by the hospitality industry. Typically custom-designed for proprietary application, these systems have not always been successfully integrated.

In the past hotel owners and management companies would buy products from technology vendors specializing in one area or another (front office, back office, reservations, food and beverage, sales and marketing and the like) and integrate these systems with varying degrees of success. The hospitality industry is thus beset by a multitude of technology applications offered by numerous hardware and software vendors. There are, for example, no fewer than 85 different property management Systems available to owners and managers of hotels offered by technology purveyors, some stable longterm providers to the industry, others much less so.

Meanwhile, most technology vendors continue to address individual parts of the industry's real needs with little regard to total system solutions. And hospitality companies tend to contribute to a fragmented marketplace quite simply by the way they purchase systems. It is often the case that a hotel company will buy a reservation system from one vendor, a property management system from another and a marketing system from yet another, depending on who makes the best products. And while there are proprietary "clusters" of related technology, the general fragmentation that has existed appears unlikely to change in the near future.

Even more importantly, the industry has failed to cooperate in the development of shared technologies. Moreover, little change in attitude has been evident during the past three or four years as the technology revolution continues to roll forward at an ever-quickening pace. And when a sound system solution is delivered to address an industry need, there is no mechanism for it to become an industry standard and thus picked up by others struggling with the same problem.

With the variety of applications for different parts of the business attended to by different vendors, it is not surprising that interface and integration are now major problem areas to be attended to. What some critics refer to as the industry's problem with closed architecture has undoubtedly cost the hospitality industry money, eroded efficiency and limited technology's benefits. But the race to put technology to work for the industry also leads to other questions related to global marketing to consumers, as well as the expanding customer services that will ultimately include Internet access and other technology routinely placed in guest rooms. All this, of course, comes at a cost. The choices that hospitality companies make in the technology realm will have profound impact on competitiveness and return to investors. These choices are not easy. Indeed, they may be among the most complex the industry faces.

While integrating disparate systems is an important challenge for the industry, it is fortunately a somewhat easier task today than it has been in the past. Whereas previously hotel computer systems would tend to be free-standing and require modest maintenance, we are now migrating rapidly to environments that include Windows applications and network solutions in which that middle component (the connection between the hardware and the application software) is becoming a more significant element in the system. Integration is clearly an important step into the future, with connectivity established between individual property operations, customer information systems, data warehouses and centralized management.

The question for many hotel organizations remains how to achieve the ultimate open system that can be shared at all levels, whether it is the central reservation system, individual property management system or any other operational area. Until now, the center of the universe has been the property management system, but that era is ending as companies realize that an exclusive focus on the customer must be supported by fully-integrated customer information systems. Anyone who is arguing on behalf of a closed system in this kind of an environment is arguing against the market.

Industry Standards

Not all the responsibility for integration, however, lies with technology providers. On the buyer's side there must be greater recognition of the commonality of needs regardless of the type of hotel property involved. Is it really necessary to continue to re-invent the wheel, for example, with all of the differing property management systems now available in the market? Even more, can the hospitality industry agree on technology standards, which are essential for full conformance and integration of systems? If the vendors can agree on interfaces between their products and other subsystems, the hospitality industry could benefit greatly. The lack of industry-wide standards — or a hospitality industry organization to create or endorse such standards — is clearly a stumbling block.

There may be some rationale for keeping certain applications proprietary to individual companies and their properties. But falling to support development of shared interfaces between systems is short-sighted at best. And ultimately it is not the hardware or even the software that delivers the competitive advantage it lies in what management does with the information when it gets it. Note that the successful hospitality organization of the future is one which reduces the traditional bias towards analysis with an associated increase in creativity. If the industry is to come together and buy into the development of common standards, it will require acknowledgment of this reality.

Technology Cycles

Timing is everything in technology investments. For hotel management, knowing when to invest in technology and what new developments to purchase is critical to managing the long-term cost and the benefit of investment in technology. A recent survey suggests that the hospitality industry as a whole has been more conservative than most in making technology investments. Microsoft - in concert with Lodging Magazine and Hospitality and Automation this year completed an industry-wide survey of technology applications in use and plans for the future. The survey results revealed that more than 70 percent of respondents are using property management systems word processing spreadsheet, accounting and point-of-sale applications. Fifty percent have sales and catering applications and 20 to 35 percent use presentation programmes and scheduling.

The Microsoft survey further discovered that 25 to 30 percent of respondents plan to install property management systems, e-mail, sales and catering, point-of-sale and accounting systems in the next 42 months. On the basis of these results, even the biggest supporter of efforts to systematize our processes would have to acknowledge that this industry remains far behind many others. But with the recent upturn in the industry's fortunes, together with the increased availability of technology at lower per-unit costs than ever before, there are clearly plans to increase spending.

The Microsoft-sponsored survey, in fact, went on to discover that 25 to 30 percent of respondents plan to install property management, e-mail, sales and catering, point-of-sale and accounting systems in the next 42 months. Longer term (over the next five years), 60 to 70 percent plan to install property management, office automation, accounting and sales systems, while 50 percent plan on telecom and food and beverage systems. Forty percent will add in-room applications. Even with these plans, however, there is clearly much to be accomplished in bringing the industry into the next millennium - at least from a technology standpoint.

Technology breakthroughs are generally considered to be cyclical. New applications are coming to market faster than ever before, and the time between conception and implementation grows shorter. It has been said that technology development in the industry once ran in seven- to -nine year cycles. This undoubtedly is no longer the case, however. In terms of pure technology, recycling appears to be occurring virtually every other year now. For the hospitality industry, the technology development cycle probably breaks into three- to five-year intervals.

Indeed, the next breakthroughs in hospitality technology may occur when the property management system is finally dislodged from its place at the center of hotel computer systems. The next big cycle will focus on the fully integrated system that brings customer, statistical and financial information together through an integration of property management, central reservations, data warehouse and distributed database systems. This appears to be where a number of the larger chains already are heading.

Network Centric Computing

We are on the threshold of some major breakthroughs in the use of network centric computing, an expression coined by IBM to describe the remote off-site world of data collection, information processing and system application that occurs in cyberspace. The integration of computing, telecommunications and interactive cable television to move information is driving this evolution, which will eventually create a seamless bridge for global sources of information. It is only a matter of time until the Internet evolves into a single, powerful highway of information supported by diverse technology applications, many already in development.

At the same time, the hospitality industry will also benefit from the development of intranets, internal networks built with the same standards and infrastructure as the Internet and World Wide Web. Intranets today offer the potential for streamlined and enhanced internal communication, and may be particularly beneficial for large organizations with scattered operations.

Further out on the horizon is the prospect of an outsourcing vehicle that can supply the computing service to all-comers, even single hotel property owners who otherwise face a distinct competitive disadvantage as the technology revolution passes them by. And lest the particularly demanding hotel chain be concerned about its unique needs, there should also be the opportunity within an outsourced networked system for appropriate customization at reasonable cost.

Network computing has enormous implications for marketing to customers on a global basis, as well as hotel operations. Consider the potential for the industry to connect with vendors worldwide for electronic purchasing, potentially achieving economies of scale and leveraging not yet possible. World purchasing functions will allow companies to customize their own catalogs.

Virtual channels of distribution using computer networking capabilities will also allow hotel companies to market products and services - some traditional to our industry, others not - to customers whether they are in the hotel, at work, or at home. This will require a migration from today's central reservation systems to tomorrow's customer information systems using network-centric solutions. Development of customer profiles and guest recognition will make it possible for hotel organizations to interact in entirely new ways with customers, regardless of their physical location.

Clearly, the large hotel companies will need to be the first to address questions raised by global networking capabilities and what this will mean in terms of technology investment. But for many hospitality companies presently struggling with the high cost of technology and the confusing state of our industry's technology affairs, this will not be an easy task. And the decisions will ultimately become further complicated by the opportunity to outsource certain functions into subscription-based networks.

It is unlikely that the hospitality industry will be forced to bear the entire burden for networking infrastructure. Strategic alliances with major technology companies will be the catalysts in building this capability as they become strategic providers of networking capabilities to hospitality and other industries. And as network-centric computing comes of age and a company's proprietary information is stored in cyberspace, security will become an ever-more important issue requiring solutions. Whether it is an e-mail gateway through an internal network or customer access via the Internet, network fire walls and encryption systems will be required to mitigate the concern many will have with system security.

In the final analysis, networking solutions will drive down the cost of technology investment "on-property" where hotel real estate and business interests merge. The solutions that hotel organizations will be able to choose from in terms of networking should also be less expensive than the current profile of technology spending. And we can expect that change to occur sooner rather than later, given the present rate of investment in Internet-based technologies.

Technology-Savvy Guests

Meanwhile, the hospitality industry's customers - hotel guests at large -have become increasingly dependent on technology - and more demanding in terms of in-room technology support. This is particularly true for the business traveler whose laptop computer often serves as a mobile office. Technology-driven entertainment options for guests - both business and leisure - also will require investments in the future. Indeed, Internet access will likely be a routine guest service at some point for hotel organizations seeking to remain competitive. And it is hoped we will find inexpensive reengineering solutions that will allow technology to be introduced into physical spaces without necessitating huge expenditures on rewiring and retooling of existing equipment. The signs of late are encouraging.

Both IBM and Oracle are working on low-end PC products that will provide all of the relevant network interfaces and windowing required. With prices expected in the range of $300 to $700 per device, these appliances will serve an exclusive networking function for economical use in the home. And there are more such products to come as other major technology companies go to market with similar offerings. Clearly, such devices have implications for use in hotel guest rooms. The industry has historically "mortgaged" its guest room space to third-party providers of entertainment service. In this coming wave of in-room technology, there may be an opportunity for hotel companies to become more proactive in the development and provision of in-room communications and networking solutions that will inevitably need to be provided in the hotel product of the future.

As technology evolves in our industry, we can expect customers to do more and more for themselves. This is already the case with lobby check-in kiosks and use of the Internet as an electronic travel agent to book hotel rooms. Indeed, those capabilities call into question the future of travel agents. What role will travel agents play in the face of increasingly direct customer access to the industry's reservation systems? If your title has the word "agent" in it, it is probably time to be concerned about the tightening of the direct relationship between hospitality companies and their customers, which is now being facilitated by technology.

Ultimately, customers may use Web casting devices that will allow them to create the best itinerary for travel based on a custom-designed profile. The workforce has become increasingly mobile as people work at home and from hotel rooms all over the world. In the future, it is likely that travel related companies will provide booking software modules for use by large corporate customers and individuals alike that will work on home or office computers - with customized profile information that includes hotel and airline preferences or restrictions set by company travel policies. Such a trend will increase the pressure on hospitality companies to respond with sophisticated yield management systems and marketing approaches.

Maximizing Revenue

Yield management - often today referred to as revenue optimization has come to the hospitality industry via the airline business where high-tech solutions to forecasting based on complex algorithms have generated tremendous improvements in yield. But for yield management to become truly effective in the hospitality industry, much more will need to be accomplished in terms of technology support and the interface between the market reality at the property level and the centralized reservations Systems that have now become such an important part of the industry's distribution system.

Consider what the industry was like before automation. All of the room inventory existed at the individual property level. Over the course of time, hotel companies fractionalized that inventory. Some remained at the property, while other parts moved to a central inventory or out to a global distribution system. Of the various challenges facing hospitality companies in the future, the task of bringing that inventory back to a central location is a significant one. Such an inventory would produce a single image that can be accessed by all points in the distribution system and would generate consistent information as to availability and pricing - a simple concept with tangible benefits but one that has yet to penetrate this industry. With revenue enhancement opportunities variously estimated in the five- to seven-percent range as such systems are centralized, this should be a quick win for our industry.

Telecommunications and Computing

The current state of telecommunications is confusing to most business people in those countries that are privatizing and deregulating their telecom industries. The telecom business is in a state of flux worldwide and with deregulation, we can expect more options and competitive pricing. In the United States, for example, it is conceivable that hoteliers will eventually be able to look to one vendor for all telcom needs - local, long distance, 800 number services, cellular, in-room entertainment, data services and Internet access.

In response to this prospect, we are likely to see a greater integration of the computing and telecommunications functions. Voice activation systems will soon arrive in central reservations offices, announcing the beginning of the early breakthroughs in the linking of computing and telecommunications. And as the telecom business continues to privatize and deregulate, the battle for customers will escalate. Clearly, the industry's leadership will need to keep an eye on this. It will probably take a while for all the dust to settle especially in the United States where there appears to be a free-for-all in this arena. But the end result should be lower unit pricing - an essential element for the hospitality industry as it seeks to align a seamless integration of the telecom and computer systems sides of its business. For international hospitality companies with chains of properties in countries around the world, the outlook should be more circumspect. For such enterprises the delivery of consistent basic telephone service in some countries will clearly need to precede further advancement of telecom technology.

Investment for Future

From a pragmatic view, hotel organizations vary widely in their ability and willingness to track the cycles of technology advances. Some organizations are early-adopters, while others embrace advancements after they have been already tested by others and the investment risk is reduced. Selling the newest technologies outside a small circle of early-adopters in our industry is not easy.

Because of the special relationships that exist between hotel companies and the third-party owners of the hotels they operate or between franchisors and their franchisees, selling the technology investment idea to these constituents is also a major challenge. It is essential that technology investment be sold as part of an integrated business plan where the technology is supporting the plan. In this manner there will generally be greater buy-in from otherwise cynical owners and franchisees who may have other things on their capital spending agenda.

As to the investments required for technology, we can safely predict that there will be significant demands for capital to cover technology investments in the years ahead. The quandary for investors in the hospitality industry, as indeed in many other industries, is how to balance the need to keep up with rapidly evolving technologies with the need for satisfactory returns on capital over the short term. This will require sound planning.

Technology investments must support a company's vision and long range strategy. Given the costs of these investments, no hospitality company can afford to have senior management going in one direction and the information technology function in another. While many companies remain focused on the hardware and software of the technology equation, not to be lost sight of is the critical need for technology leadership either within the organization or appropriately outsourced by a management team that understands how to manage these processes.

Technology planning cannot be cast in stone when new advances are emerging every few months. Historically, the industry has made smaller, one-time investments in technologies. In the future, there will be a need for contingencies allowing for on-going maintenance, support and upgrades. Plans will need to be revisited continually to ensure that sound, on-going investments are made - consistent with an organization's needs and what is available in the marketplace. Hotel organizations for years have recognized the importance of reserving capital to replace furniture, fixtures and equipment.

A similar approach may prove beneficial in the technology arena. FF&E reserves will begin to share prominence in the financial planning of hotel investments with I.T. (or Information Technology) reserves. Smaller, more frequently planned technology investments should generally pay higher dividends in the long run, as compared to the one-time, major investment followed by years of neglect. Further complicating the long-range planning for technology investment in an era of network-centric computing is the question of whether to invest in company-based systems or to wait for the availability of network subscription services provided by outside technology utilities. This may still be a long time in coming but given the big numbers involved for large hospitality companies, it is something to keep on the radar screen.

TAX CHALLENGES

Any hospitality company contemplating a cross-border investment should begin by developing a tax strategy that reflects a careful examination of tax laws of the home country, host country and any intermediary countries. Each country's domestic tax law (including any special tax structures) must be considered. At the same time, however, tax treaties between the relevant countries may otherwise override the applicable tax law.

A hospitality investor who is confused by the complexity of international tax law must stay focused on a specific short-term and long-term strategy. For instance, an investor operating under a build-and -sell philosophy should implement a different tax strategy than an investor making buy-and-operate investments.

An investor looking to sell property will be primarily concerned with the tax treatment of the capital gain. In contrast, an investor looking to operate the property will be primarily concerned with the tax treatment of operating profits. The tax analysis must be broad. To minimize tax exposure and thus improve overall investment returns, a tax analysis must cover three areas: the home country rules, any intermediary jurisdictions chosen because of preferential tax rules. and the country in which the investment is made. We begin at home.

Issues in Home Country

Although most sophisticated hospitality investors understand the tax laws of their own country, international investors must go one step further. They need to consider the application of those tax laws to income earned from sources outside the home country. Most countries tax foreign income differently than domestic income. Hong Kong. for example, exempts foreign source income from taxation. Other countries, including the United States, apply taxes only to the extent that income is taxed at a lesser rate outside the home country. Since foreign source income is generally given special treatment, the home country may restrict the ability of the investor to deduct expenses associated with foreign source income. Interest paid on debt incurred to make a foreign investment, for example. may not be deductible against domestic source income.

The hospitality investor should consider any special tax regimes of the home country and evaluate how the foreign source income will be treated for local country tax purposes. For instance, many U.S. investors strive to generate qualified capital gains to obtain a lower tax rate. Those U.S. investors are often surprised to learn that all of their gain from the sale of a foreign investment will be re-characterized as ordinary income from dividends. Alternatively, the hospitality investor may qualify for a tax exemption in the home country. In this case, maintaining the exemption and minimizing foreign country tax liability becomes a priority.

For example, U.S. pension funds are allowed to earn passive income such as dividends, interest, rents, royalties and capital gains without incurring any U.S. tax. Those pension funds, however, are taxed on any active income. Therefore, qualifying the income of a U.S. tax-exempt pension fund as "passive" should be a pivotal

requirement in the overall tax strategy of pension fund
investors.

In many cases, the tax treatment of an item of income
can be affected by what seem to be insignificant
modifications in the terms of a contract. For example,
franchise fees can be transformed from technical services
to royalties with only a slight modification of the
language in a franchise agreement. If the home country
allows preferential tax treatment of foreign source
income, royalties might be preferable since they are
typically sourced according to where the intangible is
used. In contrast, technical services are typically sourced
according to the location where they are performed.

Generally, income earned by an entity formed outside
the home country will not be taxed in the home country
until it is distributed in the home country. Increasingly,
however, home countries are enacting laws to tax income
generated in tax haven jurisdictions as it is earned. Some
countries-among them the United States-have adopted a
system that taxes certain types of passive income (i.e.,
interest, rents, royalties, or capital gains) as it is earned.

Other countries, such as Mexico, have adopted a
system that taxes income earned from certain blacklisted
countries, which are notorious tax havens. During 1996
and 1997, many Mexican companies were moving the
domicile of their holding companies from "tax haven"
jurisdictions, such as Bermuda, to "tax favored"
jurisdictions, such as The Netherlands.

Holding Companies

Hospitality investors may use intermediary holding
companies located in jurisdictions that have preferential
tax regimes. An intermediary holding company may

effectively serve to block the income from accrual in the home country. In other cases, an intermediary holding company is used to obtain a preferential treaty benefit for interest, dividends, royalties or capital gains that would not otherwise be available between the home country and host country. For many years, investors used a Dutch holding company to make investments into the United States as a way to obtain a reduced rate of withholding on dividends and interest. For non-treaty investors, the United States levies a 30 percent withholding tax on payments of dividends and interest. The income tax treaty between the United States and The Netherlands provided for a 5 percent and 0 percent rate of withholding for dividends and interest respectively. Since The Netherlands generally allows for an exemption for dividends and capital gains, the popularity of The Netherlands holding company was tremendous. However, in 1993, the United States and The Netherlands entered into a new treaty, which limits the ability of investors to "treaty shop" into the United States via the Dutch holding company.

Issues in Host Country

Host country taxation-the location of the investment-will most likely represent the most significant tax cost to the hospitality investor. There are several reasons for this. As discussed above, first (and probably most significant), the home country will usually limit its taxation of income earned abroad. Second, the host country will probably not reciprocate any special tax privileges that the investor enjoys in its home country. For example, a pension fund that benefits from a tax-exemption in its home country will probably not be given the same tax-exempt status in the host country, unless a special treaty provision exists.

Thus, the tax paid in the host country on profits earned will likely represent a significant tax cost.

To minimize the profits earned in the host country, the hospitality investor will want to push as many expenses into the host country as possible. For example, a hotel owner/operator may want to charge its host country subsidiary a royalty for having access to its name and worldwide reservation system. In addition, the hotel owner/operator may want to charge a management fee for strategic management services rendered by the home office.

To further minimize host country income tax liability, the investor should maximize the amount of debt incurred by the company holding the host country investment. The entire amount of interest paid on debt owed to a third party is typically deductible by the host country company, while deductibility of interest on debt owed to a related non-resident investor may be subject to limitations. As a result, the investor may want to fund a host country company mostly with debt acquired from a third party. In this way. the taxable profit of the host country company can be reduced by the entire amount of interest paid on the debt. If the interest at the time of distribution is subject to a low withholding tax by the host country, then the host country tax liability could be reduced overall.

Because of the significant reduction in taxable net profits caused by the acquisition of debt, the host country typically limits the amount of debt in comparison to the amount of equity of the host country company where the debt is acquired from a related party. For example, if a U.S. pension fund were seeking to acquire the shares of a target company resident in the United Kingdom, that pension fund would want to loan some of the acquisition funds to a newly created acquisition company resident in the United Kingdom. Interest paid by the acquisition company would be deductible against the operating profits of the target company. while the interest income would be tax-exempt to the U.S. pension fund. The tax authorities of the United Kingdom would typically limit the interest deductions to an amount that is commercially feasible.

In some cases, interest deductions in the home country may reduce tax liability more than an interest deduction in the host country. In those cases, the hospitality investor might not want to incur a debt at the host country level. Rather, the investor might benefit most by borrowing in the home country and contributing funds as equity to a holding company located in the host country to be used for the investment. Factors to consider in acquiring debt include relative tax rates (including host country withholding), foreign currency issues, interest withholding tax, host country capital tax, home country controlled foreign corporation legislation and deductibility of interest in the home country.

Income earned by a non-resident of the host country in the form of dividends, interest, rents, royalties or capital gains will likely be subject to withholding tax at the time of payment to the home country. However, tax treaties may reduce the amount of withholding tax levied on the payment.

Most host countries will tax a non-resident hospitality investor on capital gains realized from investments in real estate - or investments in host country companies that primarily invest in real estate. Typically, the seller of the property or the company owning the property will have an obligation to withhold some percentage of the sales proceeds and remit them to the host country's tax authorities. To avoid host country capital gains, investors may want to use a holding company in an intermediary country to hold each host country investment. When the hospitality investor is ready to dispose of a host country property, the investor would sell its stock of the holding company in the intermediary country to another investor. The sale of the holding company stock will almost always avoid taxation of host county capital gains.

5

Hotel Revenue Management

In today's environment revenue management is most often recognized as the central place for the practices and processes of hotel operations. It is such an integral part of a hotel, that in many cases it dictates the processes, procedures, interactions and responsibilities that support the maximization of hotel revenues. Most hotel companies today have one or more resources dedicated to the management of hotel revenues. These resources often include regional and corporate revenue directors and/or an assistant to the revenue director on the local level.

Today's practice of revenue management is commonly focused on day-to-day responsibilities which include the fundamentals of revenue management – forecasting, unconstrained demand assessment, inventory management, displacement analysis and distribution strategies such as channel management. Hotels commonly take a narrow view of revenue management that includes one point in time and focuses mainly on room revenue.

In the past, customer relationship management (CRM) and revenue management were not considered to be a good mix. That perspective is beginning to change as hoteliers now understand the benefits of looking at all the revenue earned throughout the guest's entire stay and including all outlets; not just room revenue. Many of the traditional pricing models are no longer relevant in the marketplace. Many of those models were based on setting an artificial "ceiling" on how high the rate could go.

Today, distribution and revenue management must incorporate strategies and elements of each into the other. However, it is often the case that revenue directors do not know all costs associated with distribution or how to calculate these costs. Worse yet, the focus is often on the cost of the channel and gives no consideration to the yields through each channel, such as guest spend on ancillary service offerings that flow through that channel.

Furthermore, hotels do not always have a plan for how they will maximize their desired segmentation via selling in the appropriate distribution channels. Hoteliers are recognizing that market segments as they are currently defined are becoming less and less meaningful due to the blurring lines of segmentation. Perhaps the time has come for the industry to redefine the rules of segmentation to allow for better classification of guests?

One thought is to segment by booking conditions. For example, someone booking through an opaque channel may be traveling for business or for leisure. But their willingness to accept the strict booking terms makes them a unique group of guests compared to other guests who do not want to make any prepayment and want a last minute change-and-cancellation option.

Moving forward revenue management is well positioned to expand and make innovative contributions in several areas.

One area that is gaining popularity is the concept of one-to-one revenue management. A future vision of revenue management is to attempt to identify the guest or client that would bring in the most revenue.

Hoteliers have been collecting information on customers for years in hopes of improving customer relationship management. A better understanding of our customers will allow us to better segment our customers. Customer segmentation will contribute to getting us closer to the ability to do one-on-one marketing and revenue management. This information allows input into consumer choice models, which will in turn allow prices to be set based on estimates of demand elasticity and buying propensity by customer segment.

For the resort, gaming and ultra-luxury market, the focus on the total revenue a guest can contribute has been the desired measurement for many years. In those environments, often the focus is not on room revenue but rather on other sources of revenue such as casino, spa, food and beverage, golf and other services the hotel offers.

The future of revenue management will include a focus on the revenue per available guest (RevPAG) and CRM. Perhaps the next generation of revenue management systems will create an offer based on the value of each individual customer. This is in contrast with today's singular focus on the room-only biased measure of RevPAR.

Function room yielding is another area that will see more focus in the future. Today, most of the processes to analyze the best group fit and catering opportunities are considered antiquated. A majority of hotels are still using a "big function book" or some variation of an automated function book, to look up the space availability and are maximizing the space, based on the manual rules within the department. The future will ideally offer a sophisticated revenue management system that maximizes the group fit and catering opportunities in much more detail and with a higher level of sophistication.

Displacement has been a very challenging exercise for function room analysis. It is challenging to determine what to negotiate when considering booking a group with a significant lead time, because when compression does hit, it is possible that more money could have been made by waiting and taking the last-minute groups that are willing to pay higher prices. But that requires hotels taking significant risks and gambles.

Because there are fewer statistical data points, it is more difficult to revenue manage function space. Thus the science is more challenging to replicate in a system. Much development is currently being focused in this area by both large hotel companies and revenue management system vendors. It is expected that much improvement will be seen during the next five years.

Analysis of channel cost is yet another area that will become more of a focus. Due to the differing costs for each distribution channel and the difference in buying behaviors of their customers, different revenue streams do not net the same profit. The process will soon shift from revenue management to a more advanced concept of optimizing profits and managing higher yield demand. Furthermore, the cost of acquisition, including sales overhead, will be included more often in the cost of a booking.

Some hotel companies are tracking profit per available room (ProfPAR) for their hotels and others are willing to sacrifice average daily rate (ADR) share (as defined by Smith Travel Research) if the group opportunity generates additional profit through ancillary spend.

Therefore, the future of market share reports will need to include ProfPAR measures in order to determine if a property is effective in generating their share of profit.

Additionally, it is predicted that employee reward models will be changed. It is important that the manner in which hotels reward employees be based on the right measurements and that employees be rewarded appropriately. Anyone who has an impact on revenues should be rewarded based on profit optimization. More incentive should be given for need times versus non-need days.

There is room in the future of revenue management for more sophisticated revenue management capabilities as mentioned. However, the industry needs to recognize that there is a gap between the advancement of these opportunities and the technology that exists to support them. The wider the gap, the slower the adoption rate. As the demands in this area continue to grow and evolve, it becomes more apparent that it is not feasible to handle revenue management via human assessment alone. At some point, a computer system needs to be part of the equation. But revenue management will always be both an art and a science – requiring both expert human resource and advanced technological systems to maximize profit.

CRITERIA FOR EVALUATNG REVENUE MANAGEMENT SYSTEMS

In anticipation of implementing a new system or upgrading an existing one, some criteria should be established in order to evaluate the potential ROI of individual Revenue Management Systems and their suitability for the objectives of one hotel or a hotel company. Many companies do this by assembling a team of key staff members from the corporate office and managers of different departments from selected properties. Their mission is to develop a framework for identifying the key functionalities expected from a Revenue Management System and a blueprint for implementing it. This gives each property and department a role in defining the objectives and expectations of the system and so should encourage buy-in from all of those that the system will impact. Some of those evaluation criteria are:

— *Who needs to know what and why?* In other words, what does each department want to see in terms of reports and other pertinent data in order to make decisions? What is the minimum required by each department and what is the optimal requirement?

— *The Current Revenue Management System.* If you currently have a revenue management system, why are you considering replacing it? Is it all of the system that you want replaced or are there certain functionalities that you would like to "add" to it? Is it more cost effective to start from "ground zero" or to purchase "add ons?"

— *Channel Management.* Most systems do this adequately. How sophisticated a system you require is dependent upon the complexity of your business mix. Will the system allow you to evaluate different channels revenue streams or are all of them dropped into the same basket?

— *Managing Multiple Revenue Sources.* How well does the system manage and evaluate revenue from unique revenue sources? For example, a property with a water park in addition to the usual hotel revenue sources needs to be able to manage the park's revenues effectively and evaluate business that maximizes revenue to all departments. A property with a popular spa needs to evaluate how the revenues of both are interrelated and manage both the inventory of rooms and spa services.

— *Analyzing and Predicting Customer Behavior.* How will the system incorporate customer behavior into its forecasts? Can it provide reports of customers' decision making timelines by market segment so that Marketing can use it to target campaigns? Will the data enable Customer Relationship Management to catch the repeat guest at the right time with the right offer at the right price?

— *What are the Benefits for Smaller Properties?* Is the system under consideration "scalable" — can some parts of the system be implemented without purchasing more functionality than necessary? Will the benefits deliver an appropriate ROI on the investment? Will the modules of a new system interface with those of the system already in place?

— *Will the Corporate Office Have Access to the Individual Hotels' Systems?* In many companies, the situation exists where the skill sets of the property Revenue Managers vary from hotel to hotel. Will a system "level the playing field" allowing the corporate revenue manager to support those properties whose managers are less proficient?

— *How Will the System Evaluate Group Business?* Many sales people complain that they have been relegated to booking groups only on the weekends and the revenue managers conversely complain that sales only wants to sell "cheap" rooms. How will the system enable the sales department to make good group bookings that satisfy the requirements of the hotel's revenue management strategy and the sales persons' desires to meet their goals? How finely can the system "drill down" the data to enable the decision making process in RFPs and contracts?

— *Can the System Manage Demand within a Geographic "Cluster?"* Some hotel companies have multiple properties within close geographic proximity to each other. Can a revenue management system assist in the redistribution of demand so that all of them can maximize their revenue based on geographic demand?

INTEGRATION OF REVENUE DRIVERS

Revenue drivers are defined as all areas of revenue generation within the organization. This includes central reservations, property-level reservations, the sales department, the electronic distribution channels and the web site. While franchised properties have a higher level of consistency through the GDS, it still requires monitoring and management at the company or property levels.

At a recent sales seminar, participants expressed frustration that they are largely unaware of, nor are they consulted about the rates that are posted on the electronic distribution channels. One result is a very high attrition rate in meetings and conventions as attendees book their hotel at these lower rates and "fall" off the group block. Another consequence is when the rate posted is lower than what has been negotiated with third-party suppliers such as wholesalers.

A coaching client of mine expressed frustration over his lack of consultation in the development of the new property web site and the rates that are being quoted through the site. First of all, the content was skewed to a specific market segment that was not representative of the core business segment and secondly, the copy changes disrupted the optimization strategy.

Secondly, the rates that were quoted were not at all aligned with the rates being quoted at the property level or through the central reservations agent and many room descriptions were inaccurate. The end result was that not only was this hotel nowhere to be found on the key word searches in the major search engines — a potential disaster for this independent property, but fewer reservations were being made through the site.

Collaboration across all departments that generate revenue is the only way to ensure continuity. This need not be a tedious process of endless meetings. A few things put into place and adjusted periodically, based on market conditions and forecasts, are sufficient:

— *Product/Rate Positioning*: A plan for product/rate positioning is ideally developed as part of the Business/Marketing plan process and includes consideration of the product/rate positioning of the competitive set, group bookings, rate resistance input from reservations and past history. Once the strategy is developed, it then only needs to be adjusted periodically. Don't forget to monitor the franchise yield management system in light of groups or events in previous years that may not be a factor in the present year.

— *Existing and Anticipated Contracts*: These include group contracts, volume contracts with LNRs, wholesalers and any other rate commitments. Just as the sales department makes decisions based on the rate structure, so should consideration be given to any agreements made thorough sales. It is one thing to adjust rates on the web site or distribution channels to drive volume at a slow time but if it undermines the agreements above, it is counter productive.

— *Web Site Presence and Reservations*: Many leisure customers locate the hotel through key word searches on the search engines. Others locate the hotel on the electronic distribution channels then access the hotel's proprietary web site. Still others will pick up the phone after visiting both and call reservations to see if they can cut a better deal. It is essential that the "message" of rate and offering be relatively consistent across all channels to be effective. The rates on the web site need to be adjusted in tandem with the electronic distribution channels and reservations needs to be aware of what's appearing on both.

Another consideration in web site development is the increased use of the site as a sales tool. It becomes the electronic brochure. The sales department's inclusion in its development is essential to the site's secondary role as the electronic brochure. Sales people should be accessing the site with their clients to moderate the virtual tour. If there is a special rate posted that is inconsistent with the rates sales are quoting, it blows them out of the water and appears to the client that the hotel doesn't know what it is doing.

The process of collecting the information is about communication and collaboration and can be accomplished through periodic updates from the revenue drivers to the revenue management team. This swings both ways as revenue management needs to keep the revenue drivers informed of their proposed tactics in order to solicit input and buy in.

The consequence of not doing this is to present an inconsistent message to the public who is in the position of making selections without any direct contact with the property thus depriving the hotel from any opportunity to make adjustments or explain the disconnect. In the consumer's mind, a hotel that can't get its act together to project consistent rates may have the same problem when it comes to servicing them as guests.

HOTEL REVENUE MANAGEMENT AND MARKET SEGMENTATION

The approach of forecasting by segment began in the airline industry - where it is common to forecast the demand for different fare products. Airline fare products are designed with specific market segments in mind. Fare products generally carry restrictions (e.g., Saturday stay over, 14-day advanced purchase) that are designed to limit eligibility to specific targeted market segments. These restrictions, also referred to as "fences," are designed to minimize "slippage" or "dilution" by members of one market segment into a lower-priced product constructed for another, more price-sensitive market segment. With the exception of one advance-purchase rate product offered by Marriott, it is uncommon in the hotel industry to have rates available to the general retail public with rules-based airline style fences.

The common array of hotel rate products includes "retail" rates and "qualified" or "entitlement" rates. Retail rates are those that are available in response to the question, "What rates are available for next Wednesday night?" Whether asked via the telephone or an online booking engine, the retail requestor is distinct from the "entitled" requestor-who is eligible for a specific rate by virtue of employment or membership in a segment, club (e.g., automobile club member), or other affiliation or qualification (e.g., senior citizen).

Advanced Market Segmentation

Rather than forecast by market segment or rate product, the best practice in yield management goes further and forecasts by the value of each rate. For example, if a hotel has five retail rate products, each with single and double occupancy rates, a system should forecast the market's willingness to pay each of those rates.

Indexing to the Competitive Environment

All hotel revenue management systems optimize based on the relationship between forecasted demand and remaining capacity. Some other industries also incorporate competitive data in their calculations. These industries, such as airlines, have reliable access to competitive pricing data. Astute hotels in our industry traditionally "shop" competitors by making telephone inquiries in the guise of reservation requests. With the advent of web-based booking engines, it is possible to "shop" competitors electronically. In some markets this works well. In other markets, web rates are not representative of rates available via other distribution channels.

Nevertheless, whether done electronically or by telephone, hotels do shop one another. Revenue management solutions should provide a mechanism for adjusting rate availability in real time based on the findings of these shopping calls. Competitor pricing can have an effect on both your hotel's demand and on the market's perception of the value of your rates. If available competitive rates for a specific stay pattern are higher than yours, some portion of competitive demand will "spill" and appear as demand for your hotel.

Indifference Rates

Every rate product has an "indifference rate" schema that may vary in large or small amounts from the corresponding quoted rates. The indifference rate is a measure of the real financial or strategic value of a particular rate. As an example, if your hotel sells a weekend rate of $159 that includes breakfast, the indifference rate might actually be $149 for single occupancy and $139 for double occupancy. These indifference rates reflect the estimated cost of the breakfast at $10 per person.

It is not uncommon for a hotel to intentionally give an indifference rate that is not based on financial calculations but has an underlying strategic justification. Suppose your hotel is located in a state capitol. The rate product associated with the government segment has a low rate that would often be closed during weekdays in peak demand seasons. Since the government segment exhibits significant demand during the lower-demand season, you decide to intentionally give the government rate product an inflated indifference rate. You justify this in hopes that providing greater availability to your rooms during times of high demand will encourage loyalty that will keep government guests coming when demand is low.

Indifference rates in a yield management system gives you the ability to customize the apparent value of particular rate products for yield management purposes. This is important both to accurately reflect the real financial value of rate products and to assign a strategic value when appropriate.

Yieldability

Yield management systems should support three states of yieldability:

Fully Yieldable: Rates are subject to rate hurdles, rate thresholds, and system generated stay controls.

Non-Yieldable: Rates are not subject to either rate hurdles or TLP-generated stay controls. If there are available rooms, non-yieldable rates can be sold.

Stay Pattern Yieldable: Rates are not subject to rate hurdles but are subject to system generated stay controls. If the top retail rate is open, then any rate designated as Stay Pattern Yieldable remains open-regardless of the prevailing rate hurdle.

The third of these three yieldability statuses allows the hotel to enter into "last room availability" contracts and still yield manage them from a stay pattern standpoint. In other words, when system optimization closes Tuesday one-day stays to allow Tuesday's remaining capacity to support longer stays, last room available rates would also be closed for a Tuesday one-day stay pattern. Therefore, rate products that fall outside the control of other yield management systems can be controlled by stay patterns.

In order to implement this yieldability feature, yield management systems should further refine the rate value forecast into separate forecasts for each rate value by yieldability status. In this way, the systems also optimizes the mix of fully yieldable and stay pattern yieldable demand.

A market segment approach to hotel yield management opens or closes entire segments or rate products at one time. One future vision of hotel revenue management goes even further. It speaks to a day when each guest is a market segment of one and the availability of rates for a requested stay would depend on a guest's past history or forecasted future with the hotel or brand. One can imagine lower room rates being available to guests with a history of dining in the hotel when compared to those that dine out. Similarly, requestors who demonstrate ongoing hotel or brand loyalty might have lower rate requirements than others without such a history.

REVENUE MANAGEMENT FOR HOTEL GMS

General Managers have vastly different levels of understanding the revenue management process. In this year of opportunity, what a general manager doesn't know and understand can jump up and bite him or her you know where. If you as a GM fall into the first category or anywhere close, a speedy ramp up on revenue management is critical to your property maximizing the revenue that ultimately becomes the basis for your bonus or incentive.

There is a feeling on the part of many GMs that Revenue Management is simply the old yield management concept repackaged. Yield management is part of it but it is far more complex than that and advances in the discipline are morphing at light speed.

Revenue Management is more complex than ever and changes in the discipline are morphing at light speed. RM not only manages demand during peak periods but also has a huge impact on stimulating demand in shoulder seasons. RM no longer only applies to room revenue but to managing the potential revenue for all profit centers. It enables a smart Customer Relationship Management strategy that has the potential to stimulate demand from the most valuable guests.

The position of the General Manager is one of juggling competing priorities, keeping the department heads from seriously hurting each other and at the same time trying to produce an exceptional guest experience. What's a GM to do to ramp up the Revenue Management IQ? Below are a few areas to test your RM IQ.

— *Understand the Reports.* Your Revenue Manager probably produces a plethora of reports and proudly gives them to you during the Revenue Management meeting. The reports come from various sources including the PMS, the GDS, the various channels and franchise reports. The Revenue Manager has probably designed a few of their own. Stare at them until they begin to make sense, ask for explanations and don't pretend that you understand them when you don't.

— *Daily, Weekly and Monthly Disciplines.* This is key to understanding what your Revenue Manager does all day. There is a set of activities that need to be performed at these intervals. Know what they are – how else can you measure how well the Revenue Manager is executing the RM strategy.

— *Channel Management.* We now refer to channels as all sources of reservations. If you still think this refers only to the Internet travel sites, you need to ramp up. Managing these channels is more than just turning the inventory and rate faucet on and off, it also includes merchant agreements, internet specials, GDS marketing etc, to stimulate demand. This is a critical area for your Revenue Manager.

— *Web Site.* Especially if you are managing an independent hotel or resort, you as a GM need to understand site design, optimization and Internet marketing. This is critical to the success of any independent. Your Revenue Manager should be intimately involved with the design and functionality of the reservation engine on your site.

— *Rate Strategy versus Pricing Strategy.* The rate strategy is where you position your rate structure for the year or fiscal period. The pricing strategy includes closing discounts, rates for 'hot dates' etc., in the short term or within the period covered by the rate strategy.

— *Revenue Management and Customer Relationship Management.* This tends to produce the glazed over 'deer in the headlights' look. The simple explanation is that CRM is about identifying the value of customers, individually or by market segment and then developing relationships with them in order to secure their loyalty or, put simply, repeat business. It can be this simple or much more complex but GMs need to understand what this means and the implications for the future.

The above is a short list of some of the basics that all GMs need to have a grasp of even if their Revenue Manager is supported by a Corporate Revenue Manager – remember it is your hotel's revenue for which you are ultimately responsible and compensated for.

MANAGING LABOUR COSTS

Due to the magnitude of the expense, labour costs and issues have always consumed a substantial portion of the time and efforts of hotel managers. Now, with news of union contact negotiations, changes to immigration laws, and proposed legislation to increase the minimum wage, hotel managers are on edge.

Several political and economic factors are brewing that may have a strong influence on hotel labour costs.

— Union contract negotiations are under way in several major cities.
— Proposed changes to immigration laws could affect the ability of hotels to find and retain employees.
— Local and state governments are proposing legislation to increase the minimum wage.

Labour costs are comprised of two major components; salaries and wage, and employee benefits. In the past three years, the rise in employee benefits has outpaced the growth in salaries and wages. Employee benefits include items such as payroll taxes, payroll-related insurance, subsidized employee insurances and meals, and retirement plans.

Labour is considered a semi-variable cost. Base staffing levels, plus management salaries, make up the fixed component of labour costs. The majority of jobs in the typical hotel are filled by hourly rate employees, and thus their cost is a direct function of the volume of business. The payroll for these employees is the variable component.

In the hotel industry, lodging facilities are frequently defined by the level of service they provide to their guests. Due to the extensive services and amenities offered at resort and convention hotels, these property types have the highest payroll ratios as a percentage of total expenses.

While managing labour expenses is important, hotel managers are also aware that employees are an integral part of the lodging experience. The interaction between hotel guests and employees has a dramatic impact on the customer experience and the success of the business operation.

The current economic climate in our industry requires that we improve efficiencies in all segments of operations. Labour represents the largest single component of operating expenses – easily comprising up to 50% of a hotel's operations. Understanding labour costs on a daily, weekly and monthly basis would allow you to manage your labour costs and productivity indicators more effectively. However, there are very few tools designed to facilitate labour analysis, with most financial professionals relying on large, cumbersome spreadsheets, which are difficult to manage and prone to error.

priZem International Inc. (pZi) is the hospitality industry's premiere source for financial consulting and technology solutions. Using a comprehensive suite of services and hosted applications, pZi provides clients with the tools necessary to maximize revenues while minimizing costs. pZi has developed *Labour Intelligence,* a labour reporting database for management that offers financial professionals the ability to perform in-depth analysis of labour costs and needs on a daily, weekly and monthly basis. *Labour Intelligence* is a simple tool that also offers in-depth analysis of labour costs as compared to revenues on a daily, weekly and monthly basis. This easy-to-use software will help management administer labour costs as compared to forecast, budget and prior year as well as help manage employee schedules based on service volume and demand. With pZi's intuitive tool, you will be able to assess and revise labour requirements to provide hotel operators with the information they need to shift labour forces and reduce costs quickly and efficiently.

pZi is a hospitality consulting group formed in 1999 to help fill the gaps in financial and technology operations within the hospitality industry. Its *Labour Intelligence, Market Intelligence* and *Budget Intelligence* applications were designed by those same hospitality professionals who have more than 20 years experience each in Finance and Technology within the hospitality industry. By bringing their experience together, they have developed simple, cost effective tools that can help fill those crucial and often unnoticed gaps.

The primary purpose of *Labour Intelligence* is to allow management to generate useful and insightful reports. With pZi's tool, you will be able to:

— Provide corporate management with the ability to evaluate labour cost from one central location.

— Measure current key performance indicators against historical key performance indicators

— Help establish property labour standards

— Export data to any spread sheet or budget programme

— Interface to any time clock

Labour Intelligence provides detailed historical labour data that provides important information needed to:

— Remove the weak link created by the common use of manual, inefficient and error-prone spreadsheets

— Provide hotel operators with the information needed to shift labour forces and reduce costs quickly and effectively

— Allow management to properly determine how associated costs compare to forecast, budget and prior year.

Linking Staffing, Labour and Budgets

Hotel budgets are done every year and all of them address revenues, expenses and labour costs. For many companies, the budget is a one-time a year exercise that focuses on analyzing past costs and projecting future costs. Many organizations use comprehensive spreadsheet models that incorporate basic principles of flex budgeting. In the most successful processes, senior and middle management participate so that all involved understand how the budget was constructed and what the underlying assumptions are.

Once the budget is complete, actual performance is analyzed relative to budget each month. Assumptions are reviewed and questioned, and may even be revised if the results are satisfactory. Unfortunately, too many organizations settle for the annual and periodic reviews. Cost management needs to be a daily and weekly endeavor, especially where labour is concerned.

Reviewing labour costs at the end of the month does not go far enough in helping managers control costs. The process is too dependent on senior management reviewing results and asking middle management to explain what happened. For labour management to be effective, department heads need to receive regular information that helps them plan and critique information. The information system must be designed to operate at both the senior and middle level, giving all involved individuals essential information.

To accomplish this, the budget and 'labour management processes need to be integrated. The labour standards that drive the budget must be available for weekly planning and analysis. While this approach is common for hotel housekeepers, it's not sufficiently widespread to meet the needs of all departments. Too many labour categories are budgeted as a percent of revenue rather than in either hours per day or hours per unit (or units per hour).

Labour budgets need to be developed using standards that the manager can understand and manage to. Food staffing (kitchens, stewards, servers) should be budgeted based on covers per hour. The department manager needs to be able to manage labour based on covers per hour for the day, week and month. If staffing standards are available in covers per hour but the budget does not use the same approach, there will be discrepancies in performance. And the same is true if the budget includes covers per hour but there's no system in place to help the manager plan and analyze performance using the same measurements.

Certainly, average check (and average unit price) is of concern to all. However, shortfalls in average unit price need a different solution from problems with productivity. A budget (or a labour standard) that does not reflect the different challenges posed by managing revenue and managing costs does not help an organization manage costs effectively.

To effectively manage labour, the tools and system must make staffing standards available for short term planning and analysis. There should be an information system that allows managers to develop a Labour plan based on the forecasts and that tells them how well performance compared to standard daily and weekly. This helps them constantly critique and refine labour use. It also positions them to tell senior management how they're doing rather than, as is so often the case, waiting for senior management to review a report and ask questions.

The same standards should be incorporated into the periodic and annual budgeting. Integrating the processes ensures that middle management is properly positioned to manage performance. This creates an environment in which information is shared and used by all involved to improve performance throughout the year.

Improving Labour Costs

In today's business environment labour is both a key to driving revenue growth and the largest cost item in the operating budget. The average full-service hotel spends between 32 percent and 36 percent of revenue on direct labour. Because labour represents such a large percentage of the cost base at the property level, improving labour efficiency represents a tremendous opportunity for profit improvement. However, it would be a mistake to consider a labour project strictly as a cost reduction opportunity. A plan to manage labour costs should not be about reduction. It should be about establishing a mechanism to continually ensure an organization has the right amount of labour in place to provide the necessary level of service.

More often than not, labour is viewed purely from the cost perspective and often adjustments result in negative impacts on guests, employees and ultimately the shareholder. A more effective approach is to take a strategic view of labour costs to ensure that all aspects of labour management are taken into account. The result is a broader approach that takes into account key areas of impact:

— Guest service levels and guest satisfaction

— Internal service levels

— Employee satisfaction and retention

Understand Objectives. Make sure objectives are determined at the start of the project. These will likely focus on cost reduction expectations, integration of service standards and the impact on employee satisfaction. Organizations need to incorporate a balanced approach and not just focus on the cost aspect in order to generate results that are sustainable.

Executive Sponsorship and Support. It is imperative that executives buy into the objectives and will support the development of the plan. Support and buy-in from operations is especially crucial.

Visibility Is a Necessity. In order to continually manage the improvements made to labour management capabilities, an organization must be able to review labour cost figures on a timely basis and down to a level that is meaningful such as by property, by department, by shift and by labour classification. This will require that a process be developed to gather, analyze and distribute labour cost information in a timely manner.

Make Competition a Factor. Internal benchmarking and comparisons of each property on the basis of defined, comparable labour metrics can be very powerful. Once department heads know that their numbers will be compared with their peers and included in performance measurements, they look for every improvement opportunity available. A key to this is using a balanced set of performance metrics that encompass not only cost but also guest and employee satisfaction.

Skill Assessments and Effective Training. A very important and necessary factor in the effectiveness and efficiency of an organization's labour force will be their mastery of the required skill sets. Identify the competencies that are required for each position at each level. Evaluate employees and design and implement the needed training programmes. The cost of this effort will typically be returned many times over through labour productivity gains. While tighter labour management can be viewed as a negative by employees — it actually is quite the opposite. Employees gain by knowing what is expected of them, avoiding the frustration of performing a job they are not well trained for and by having a schedule they can count on and that suits their needs. Additionally, the better the company is doing financially the more secure the employee is and the better the opportunity to participate in the rewards.

Effective Labour Management

A project methodology that can be quite effective in establishing a focused programme for labour management should include the following:

— Eliminate any unnecessary work through process reviews, activity analysis and other means including the review of best practices.

— Review the organizational structures in the identified areas for opportunities to improve effectiveness.

— Once processes and organizational structures are optimized, labour standards and the accompanying management processes will need to be established. The resulting labour standards must be beta tested at a selected group of properties with the appropriate level of monitoring, adjustment and reporting.

— Based on the resulting labour standards, an implementation plan must be established that will include the resulting labour standards and an action plan to implement the standards across the organization.

— Prior to rollout the organization should ensure that a mechanism to forecast the need for labour is in place. This is critical to making effective use of labour productivity standards.

— Additionally, automation of the scheduling process is necessary to achieve the full benefits of labour productivity standards. There are several impressive labour scheduling systems available. Selecting a package that best matches the specific needs of an organization is important.

— Finally, labour analytics provided to key information points are necessary to effectively maintain and continually improve labour cost. An organization will need to design the process and mechanism to distribute the information in a timely manner.

Whatever methodology is pursued there are steps an organization can take to avoid some of the common pitfalls of a labour management project.

Many organizations have fewer employees than they did nine months ago. Take advantage of it. Implementing improved labour management techniques will be easier and more manageable with a smaller workforce and will help maintain efficiency as the organization ramps back up.

6

Hospitality E-business Strategies

E-business and its applications are undoubtedly the major topic in the boardrooms of most of the world's largest companies. The financial markets are making massive investments in the companies that deliver Internet technologies, content and related products and services, and the corporate world is now moving toward e-business offerings at a rapid clip. On the business-to-business (b-to-b) front, e-business is projected to grow enormously in the United States over the next several years, with business-to-consumer (b-to-c) trade not as big, but growing just as fast.

E-business is rewriting the economic rules globally for every industry—including hospitality, travel and leisure. Indeed, it's important to recognize that we are now operating in what has been described as the "new economy," as global trends drive change, including globalization, consolidation, convergence, technology and communications. Even more, it is clear that the underlying sources of value are also changing. Use of intangible assets such as information, brands, customers, relationships and networks distinguish the most successful companies in the world.

IMPACT OF THE INTERNET TECHNOLOGY

It is clear that the Internet is having a huge impact on how we conduct our lives and our businesses. And it arrived virtually overnight. In the United States, for example, it took 38 years for television to get into 50 million homes. For the Internet, it took just five years. And for those U.S. consumers that are online, four out of five believe that the Internet is a more important invention than television. Of these same online consumers, close to six in 10 prefer e-mail to paper mail for business correspondence and over one in four check their e-mail while on vacation.

The Internet is also changing the customer relationship—undermining and redirecting customer attention to new sellers of products and services and away from their traditional relationships. And as this occurs, the traditional approaches that hospitality businesses have taken to distribution are all being affected. From reservations taken over the Internet, which are projected to more than double to 9% of volume over the next year, to the declining role of the travel agent.

This occurs as so-called "infomediaries" provide information and access, and software robots troll the activity online to develop matches between buyers and sellers, analyzing complex patterns and looking for trends for marketers to capitalize upon. As for the infomediaries, we can expect some of these to move into the transactions business and continue the process of disintermediation. For some hospitality companies, it may be best to join this new competition, particularly if it cannot be beaten at its own game.

The reality today is that the balance of power is shifting from sellers to buyers and in so doing it makes the importance of delivering high-quality service, convenience and value for money ever more compelling. The Internet has clearly leveled the playing field by making price information broadly available to the consumer. Internet business models affect product and services offerings, pricing, distribution and customer service, as well as long-term information capabilities. As a consequence, some hospitality suppliers will inevitably feed different tranches of their inventory through the various channels at their disposal—including the Internet, travel management organizations, destination packagers and the like.

In the end, customers want both convenience and consistency. They don't have all the leisure time that futurists once predicted they would have by now. In fact, they have less. Today's fast-paced world produces ever more stress, and consumers want information and they want it fast. And if hospitality companies and travel providers don't deliver convenience, somebody else inevitably will. They also want to be wired up to the rest of the world—at home, in their office and especially when they travel. And for hoteliers trying to cope with in-room technologies and the delivery of high-speed Internet access, we will soon be seeing more integration of network communication and entertainment products to further complicate or liberate our lives, depending on your point of view. Customers are also looking for consistency. In the emerging networked world, aligning the value propositions of alliance partners and ensuring a seamless and consistent experience will only be as good as the weakest link in the chain.

NEW BUSINESS RULES

Within this new economy, the operating environment for hospitality companies is changing. There are new rules of conduct, new relationships and new criteria for success, along with a new set of metrics. The revolution that we must now confront is therefore no less significant than the one that our forebears had to deal with as the Industrial Revolution changed how people lived, worked and dealt with each other. And like our distant relatives of centuries ago, there are boundless opportunities and countless risks, most obscured within an environment of great uncertainty. In such an era there are certain traits to business behavior that will distinguish success from failure. At this stage in the new economy's evolution, these traits would appear to include speed, agility and flexibility.

Speed is necessary to get to market early with a first-mover advantage that assures early adoption by an increasingly fickle, restless and frequently disloyal customer. Such speed is imperative as so-called "start-up" companies come to dominate their chosen niche in extremely short periods of time, frequently preempting the opportunity for those too slow to react.

Agility is required to be able to respond to competitive threats by not only those we know and can monitor, but also unseen competitors. These latter competitors may not even exist as yet, but as they emerge, they may quickly disintermediate established customer relationships.

And, finally, flexibility is needed to reorganize the established models of business and all of the related processes, and adapt the organization in organic fashion to a new environment in whatever form it takes.

For business executives at large, one of the most compelling changes that has confronted them in recent years is the potential for e-business. But while the significance of these new media are all too apparent, the business solutions required to capitalize on opportunities they offer are unfortunately not. For most hospitality executives, the essential frame of reference has been a geocentric one where real estate and geography have been the big drivers in a physical world—buildings, dots on maps, markets served, chains. In tomorrow's world, these concepts will require some fundamental adjustments to provide for market "spaces" rather than "places" as the nature of relationships between hotel businesses, their customers, their suppliers and their alliance partners go through rapid and constant change.

As these changes occur, the new economy's business leaders must quickly learn the new rules of the game and adjust their approaches accordingly. And the most successful among us will align key processes around the Internet, build corporate intelligence automatically, create integrated value chains and develop new processes to deal with an ever-changing set of circumstances.

HUMAN CAPITAL CHALLENGE

Supporting the changes in the new economy will be a vast pool of talented human capital anxious to bring new ideas and new technologies to bear on the traditional ways of doing business and, in doing so, steadily increase the pace of productivity improvement. And if the hospitality industry is to respond to this coming reality, it will need to address some of its most vexing challenges— particularly those relating to the recruitment, training and development of human capital. The human capital inventory for an e-business will require entrepreneurship, as well as visionary leadership, strength in sales and marketing and commitment to customer relationship management. The organizational bias will need to be toward creativity and risk-taking, and away from dependency on analysis and procedures. In addition to the human capital challenge, many of today's legacy organizations are better structured to work in the old economy, but are considerably less aligned for many activities in the "new." The cultural challenges may in fact be no less daunting than those presented by some of the technological ones. For large organizations attempting a major shift in orientation, the presence of a significant culture may turn out to be quite a hindrance.

REDEFINING THE HOSPITALITY BUSINESS

In some industries, profits are made on spare parts and maintenance rather than on mainstream products. In the new economy, we may see this business model replicated in the hospitality industry. And for those companies that discount or give away products such as hotel rooms in order to sell linked services, they surely will be redefining the meaning of hospitality. They will also be marketing an array of hospitality and leisure products and services to a customer base that is no longer satisfied with the traditional ways of making such purchases.

Hospitality businesses that traditionally provided room, board, management and marketing may need to rethink their roles in the new economy, particularly as services become more valuable than products. With the rapid growth of "infomediaries" and their facilitation of transactions, hospitality businesses may need to redefine themselves in order to prosper in an increasingly electronic world where one-to-one customization is the order of the day. But for those contemplating repositioning their companies in an e-business environment, it will be necessary to focus on the current value proposition of the business and determine how it might be reformatted or enhanced to ensure success in the new setting.

As information technology (IT) is used to facilitate a company's entry into the world of electronic commerce, our industry's leadership will also need to overcome a natural tendency to be disappointed by the role of IT in achieving competitive advantage. For many years IT was seen as a mechanism to support back office finance and accounting functions. In the future, it inevitably will be one of the principal drivers of value creation in the new economy. But we should not be mislead by IT—in e-business, it will be the strategy, not the technology that will make the difference between success and failure. But having the strategy in place is only the first step. It must be linked to every part of the business.

PLANNING FOR E-BUSINESS

With the costs of playing in the e-business world escalating rapidly, hospitality executives should consider the four phases of what might be called the "E-Business Lifecycle." The first of these—E-Business Strategy Development and Planning—must address the market and competitive context, articulate the vision and opportunity, outline the strategy and the business case, and identify the risks. In recent years, we have frequently seen hospitality businesses put up a Web site on the Internet and consider this an e-business strategy. But without a strategy for this new form of commerce and the business planning process to drive it, such reactionary approaches stand little chance for success.

Once the plan is in place, an e-business design phase can commence to address site design, lay out the business architecture, identify the technical infrastructure, plan for performance, availability and capacity, and deal with tax issues and enterprise security. Following the design phase, E-Business implementation will prepare for the launch with training and change enablement, implementation and integration, testing and roll-out. Once in place, E-Business Operations will need to be supported by IT and audit services, Web site activity analysis and Web site maintenance. Finally, measurement systems will need to be established to monitor performance.

As industry executives embark on this e-business lifecycle, they will need in the first stage to clearly establish the business case for investing in new technologies, systems and organizations by addressing both the cost reduction and revenue enhancement benefits. On the revenue side, there are a number of factors to consider. These include the company's ability to identify and recruit the most valuable customers; the ability to seamlessly cross-sell the company's products and services, as well as those of alliance partners; the ability to retain valuable customers and reduce attrition (especially relevant in a world of questionable brand loyalty); and finally, when and how to eliminate costly and unnecessary discounts through revenue optimization.

In this kind of environment, the property management system will no longer hold sway as the center of the hospitality universe, but will become just one in a series of customer touch-points that will increasingly include the Internet. These touch-points will ultimately need to be fully integrated into a customer information system supported by sophisticated data warehousing and data mining technologies.

Adding to the industry's costs in this portrait of the future is the cost of grafting e-business technologies onto the industry's legacy systems. At a certain stage, it may make sense to start from scratch and ensure that every system is Web-enabled. This would allow a total interface for a high-growth e-business, thereby maximizing the customer relationship management opportunities that it presents.

As to the role of the Internet, its comprehensive reach and ubiquitous nature has already ensured its central place in the new economy. But how should we evaluate whether an Internet application is deserving of our attention? Firstly, productivity on the Internet in the years to come will be vastly improved by much higher bandwidth than is currently in place. And with higher bandwidth will come applications that can benefit from such extra capacity delivering tightly focused and reliable content to an increasingly sophisticated and demanding e-customer. If an Internet application is to succeed in the future, it will therefore need to be designed to capitalize on this coming reality.

Secondly, an Internet application needs to form a community of some sort because without a sense of place, albeit of the virtual sort participants will not have that all-important sense of belonging. And as with the industrial revolution, which drew a disparate population to centers of economic activity, so will such "intranet communities" grow in value as their populations increase in size and their economic product expands.

For larger businesses that form such communities, they are developing new revenue sources and are reinventing their relationships with customers, employees, suppliers and partners. Smaller companies intent on participating in this new environment, may need to be content as a participant in an established community, rather than trying to take on the creation of a community itself. It is better, perhaps, to be one of many players in a successful space than struggling to establish an identity in a world surrounded by also-rans.

Whether large or small, community developers and marketers of the virtual sort will have to recognize that what may have appeared cool in the physical world to generations brought up in the old economy will not work in the world of e-business. Being cool and staying that way in order to get and keep attention will remain a constant challenge, especially for those keen to nurture a younger generation of travelers brought up on MTV and the Web.

Finally, the successful Internet application needs to improve service while reducing transaction costs, particularly as the balance of power in the buy/sell relationship continues its inexorable migration from sellers to buyers. Service improvement strategies will be nothing new for hospitality businesses, but it is noteworthy that service is the top factor that encourages return e-business. This must be an area of focus since the current growth of e-business appears destined to outpace the supporting infrastructure and its related service at least over the short term. But as hospitality executives know, delivering good service can be expensive. Scaling the types of service response to the circumstances is a growing need, but one that can be modulated if the value of each customer can be distinguished and the response adjusted accordingly.

E-STRATEGY PLANNING

During the past several years, e-business has changed the business paradigm and has created a new business model across all industries. This new business model is based on creating new channels that facilitate open communication among "service users" and "service providers," enabling information access, information exchange, and procurement of goods and services faster and cheaper.

Using this business model, a new breed of young companies have entered the market attracting massive investments and creating extremely high market values. These new companies have been able to effectively compete with more established and mature companies, taking away their market share, and even acquiring them. Examples of these are AOL acquiring Time Warner, and Travelocity providing air-line and hotel bookings at lower rates than classic travel intermediaries. However, since the new companies have focused on growth and not paid much attention to profitability, their long-term success is questionable, unless they can use the mature company approach of combining growth with profitability.

The emergence of these new e-business organizations has awakened the mature organizations to the need to focus on the e-business paradigm and position their own organizations to benefit from this new business model. These organizations have realized that if they can be successful in taking advantage of the e-business paradigm, they can regain market share from the new companies because they have the skills and discipline to focus on generating both profit and growth and positioning themselves ahead of their new competition.

The hospitality industry is a prime candidate for benefiting immensely from e-business. In the more distant past, the hospitality industry had been a technology leader with its comprehensive reservation systems and property management systems. Unfortunately during the past decade, this industry has not placed as much emphasis on technology as a critical factor for its future, as it did in the past. However, this industry can no longer lag behind with its technology usage. Now is the time for the hospitality industry to bridge the gap in its technology usage and embrace the

Internet and e-business. The hospitality industry has the benefit of learning from other industries' successes, as well as mistakes, and approach e-commerce with a solid e-strategy to avoid potential pitfalls that its predecessors faced.

Currently, most hospitality executives are aware of the impact of this new business model and are actively searching to find ways of incorporating e-business into their companies' operations. However, often these efforts are done reactively and without a clear strategy and plan. While this reactive approach can produce short-term benefits, it will be less effective and more expensive in the long run.

Therefore, to truly benefit from the impact of e-business, it is imperative to develop a clear strategy and roadmap that addresses all aspects of e-commerce. The market leaders are those companies that have a clear vision of how their organization will benefit from e-business, supported with a comprehensive strategy and plan. A key critical success factor for e-business is having a viable e-business strategy and plan.

There are several steps for hotel companies to consider in developing an effective e-strategy, depending on what their focus is and whether it is mainly directed to identifying and defining new markets and business opportunities or looking to e-commerce to improve the operating fundamentals of the organization.

There are a number of steps typically involved in developing an e-business strategy. Which steps to begin with depend on the focus of the initiatives. A suggested stepped approach to developing an e-business vision, strategy, and plan follows.

Stage One: E-Strategy and Branding

The first stage in developing the e-business strategy involves determining the e-business readiness of the company and preparing a high-level vision and strategy. Typical steps are as follows:

1. *Conduct a Net Readiness Assessment* — This entails a functional and technical assessment of the company's abilities to develop and deploy Internet applications in support of stated business objectives.

2. *Prepare a High-Level Business Strategy* — A plan should be developed for using the Internet for competitive advantage and growth based on the business's goals, objectives, competitive environment, and culture. Key components typically include:

   — Strategic goals and objectives and corresponding metrics

   — Business vision

   — Identified e-business opportunities and threats

   — High-level initiatives definition

   — Top-level roadmap and timeline

   — Organizational roles and responsibilities

3. *Develop a High-Level System and Component Architecture* — The end-state technical vision should be developed, including cornerstone application system descriptions, proposed technical components including Web and hardware server specifications, high-level network architecture, and integration approaches.

4. *Refine the Brand Strategy and Positioning* — A strategy for managing the company's brands via Internet-based solutions should be developed.

5. *Develop a Comprehensive Business Case* — At this point it is important to develop a business case for all

opportunities identified in the business strategy. The business case may document estimates of market valuation or response to e-business initiatives, in addition to classic return-on-investment model parameters and metrics.

6. *Prepare Prototype Designs* — It is useful to develop a prototype to demonstrate functionality and reactive direction based on identified strategic objectives to illustrate the opportunity and create momentum around the chosen initiatives.

7. *Develop a Go-To-Market Strategy* — A need exists to prepare a high-level, go-to-market strategy for the e-business solutions in response to the results of customer needs and customer value assessments.

8. *Prepare a Detailed Requirements Analysis* — This involves defining the functional and technical requirements of the pro-posed business solutions.

9. *Develop Appropriate Solution Design Specifications* — Design specifications should be prepared to reflect the creative and interactive designs developed to meet the business requirements and support the brand positioning.

10. *Refine Applications, Technical, and Content Architectures* — The e-business strategy should contain a description of the underlying application integration framework and development approach, such as EJB or CORBA, as well as the major functional systems within the e-business application solution, hardware specifications, network architecture, and content specifications.

11. *Develop e-Business Process Specifications and Organizational Design* — Business processes for the new e-business model and the changes required to current processes to migrate to the new model should be identified, as well as the new e-business organizational structure for the company or venture.

12. *Determine the Hardware/ Network Infrastructure* — The physical infrastructure that comprises the production and development environments and their opera-tins should be developed.

All of these steps are the basis for an appropriated, staged, designed, and implemented e-business strategy.

Priority Areas of E-business for Hotels

While some hotel companies are successfully entering the e-procurement business and others employ Web-based reservations networks, the industry as a whole is not yet where it should be when compared to other industries. E-business is quickly spreading throughout all aspects of the business. Some of the priori-ties are briefly described.

Customer Oriented e-Business Initiatives

In the guest room, for example, guests in some hotels can use the Internet to do a variety of things: access entertainment, shop, plan tours, make reservations, and plan further travel. Several hotel companies, for instance, Hilton.com, are extending their reach to offer services and purchase options to customers outside the hotel environment through their commercial Web sites and Customer Loyalty Programme.

As hotel customers increasingly adopt a self-serve view of the world, those properties and chains that capitalize on this trend will be able to differentiate themselves from the competition and gain market share. E-business initiatives are underway to connect with and service corporate accounts as well, with proprietary Web-based programmes and services and on-line bookings of meetings and catering events.

Hotel Back-Office Functions

Another area with potential is the use of the Internet to facilitate hotel back-office functions. The financial, human resources, asset management, and other back-office needs can be effectively addressed through this new channel. Back-office managers, by out-sourcing IT infrastructure and business applications management, may no longer have to worry about maintaining their own systems or having the right technical people to sup-port them. They can "have their cake and eat it too." They can have access to what applications they need through the Internet, when and where they need it. They can focus on their core competency and be business managers who can get the data that they need to manage their operations effectively and turn their organizations into effective and profitable entities.

E-Integration of Disparate Systems

Hotel companies generally have disparate systems that support individual needs, such as reservation, property management, revenue management, financial management, human resources, payroll, sales and catering, marketing, and many more. Each of these systems is very vital to the operations of the hotel. Each hotel application stores and produces valuable data that needs to be transformed into information that various resources throughout the organization can access and use to perform their jobs more effectively.

Having consistent, accurate, and timely information can position a hotel with the information that it needs to manage itself more effectively and produce results that can increase revenue, control and reduce expenses, and finally increase profits. The Internet can serve the vital purpose of providing a foundation for integration of various systems and business applications across a wide spectrum of business constituents, including hotel companies, their franchisees, corporate customers, and dispersed business units. This is accomplished by deploying middleware solutions to link legacy back-end business applications to Web front-end applications.

Data Integration

The need to have access to the right data to manage the hotel operations is compounded for the owners of properties with multiple hotel chain affiliations. Since they use different chains' systems, being able to roll up their performance data into a single database that can be used for management and reporting purposes across all properties and chains becomes a significant critical success factor. The ultimate questions for any hotel owner or operator is how to get good customer data and how to store it in a proper repository so it can be utilized as needed. Many organizations can gather data, but don't know how to consolidate it by different names or variations, such as Bill Smith, William Smith, or W. Smith.

Furthermore, a long-standing challenge is to be able to determine who are a hotel's best customers and subsequently tailor specific services for them. For many companies, this is still an impossibility. However, in this day and age and with the new tools available in the marketplace, this should become a reality. In order to achieve the out-lined objectives of integrating data across a company or portfolio of properties, hotel companies need to integrate the data from these disparate systems, maintain the data in a single data repository, provide tools that transform the data into information, and facilitate access to the right data at the right time from any location within the hotel company.

A good vehicle to access the data from any location is the Internet or the World Wide Web. There are new tools that help with data integration, transformation, analytics, and Internet-based access. Using these tools, coupled with a thin client application, staff managers and headquarter personnel can access the right level of data that is pertinent to their need from any location. By using this approach, the dream of knowing who are the right customers can, and will, become a reality.

Single Image Room Reservations Inventory

Having an integrated environment, coupled with an integrated database, can help achieve another long-standing hospitality dream. The dream is to have a single image inventory system where the total room inventory for any major hotel entity is maintained in one place, and all reservation sources access the same database to book rooms. The value of the single image inventory system is in eliminating all unnecessary intermediary reservation steps, thus avoiding over and under bookings.

Although many claim to have this capability, it is not yet widely available. The first organization that can fully achieve this capability will enter a new era in reservations and will be able to achieve tremendous success. A number of e-business initiatives are under way to de-couple rooms inventory management from PMS applications and distribute reservation data and information over the Web from centrally hosted applications. A number of Web-based reservation services, like Worldres.com and others, are providing fully Web-based solutions for hotels.

Vertical Web Portals and Hotel Chain Extranets

The industry needs an effective Web portal, perhaps on a chainwide or even an industry wide basis, that provides operators and owners with information, tools, business applications, and industry best practices to help them run their businesses. Topics could range from labor issues, including how to hire the best people, what incentives to offer to properties for sale, the availability of service companies, and many other functions. A number of hotel chains, such as Cendant, Choice, and others, have established extranet information portals to push vital information and business tools out to franchisees. A number of hospitality industry vertical Web portals, such as VerticalNet's hospitality portal, have also been introduced recently to offer similar capabilities and information to independent hotels.

E-Procurement

E-procurement as a viable business-to-business Internet solution has taken hold in a major way in the hospitality industry. One major e-procurement consortia, Avendra, involves a joint venture between Bass Hotels, Marriott International, Hyatt, and Club Corp. These companies have pooled their buying power and are in the process of implementing an integrated catalog ordering system linking a variety of suppliers to their hotels and clubs. This is in an effort to dramatically stream-line the purchasing process.

REINVENTING HOSPITALITY BUSINESS

Hotel and travel companies have traditionally viewed technology as an enabler. Large-scale technology implementations have generally been part of efforts to design more robust business processes to reduce costs, improve quality and speed time to market. Once the opportunities are identified, teams assess the role that information technology might play in the implementation. In contrast, Internet technologies are more than enablers in the new economy. They are the drivers of entirely new business models.

The successful companies of the 20th century are beginning to understand that the marketplace of the 21st century requires them to acquire and retain a critical mass of valued customers, and they are developing new competencies to deliver new sources of value to these customers. The foundation of success increasingly is the ability to create new business models that leverage Internet technologies to deliver unique value to customers.

Diverse factors are driving the successful 20th century businesses in hospitality and travel to reinvent themselves for the 21st century using eBusiness. But the drivers of change differ in Business to Consumer (B2C) and Business-to-Business (B2B) spaces. In the B2C arena, the desire to strengthen customer relationships, develop new revenue streams, enhance profit margins and create more value are all motivating rapid change. The foundation of success increasingly is the ability to create new business models that leverge Internet technologies to deliver unique value to customers.

Internet intermediaries such as lastminute.com and travelocity.com have recently spent large amounts of marketing funds to build brand awareness. Bass plc and Starwood Hotels & Resorts Worldwide, for example, took early equity stakes in lastminute.com, which sells distressed room, flight and other inventory. The business has moved rapidly and successfully in building high levels of brand awareness out of the starting gate. Loyalty programmes targeting Web-site purchases have now evolved. This new brand awareness and loyalty is a direct threat to the decades of investment in the bricks-and-mortar brands of the industry.

As online clearinghouses appeal to a growing number of customers, they are directly challenging the hotel brands. Online purchasers may no longer be buying a Holiday Inn room - rather they may be buying a lastminute.com weekend break or a priceline.com vacation. The major brand owners have had to fight back. And aligning with competitors in the industry is often perceived to add more value than aligning with the new intermediaries.

Customers' needs do not stay the same. The hotel industry meets the core need of providing a safe and secure home-away-from-home for the business and leisure traveller. But an increasing number of guests - business and leisure, domestic and international - require high-speed Internet access and related capabilities. Guests expect remote-office (and entertainment) environments no less functional than they have at home or in the office. Recently, we have witnessed agreements being signed by Windsor Hospitality Group and Four Seasons (with Wayport, Inc.), Mandarin Oriental (with STSN) and several other chains. Under these agreements, hotels are able to offer their business and leisure clients the same levels of Internet access (speed and response, for example) that has become the norm in their offices or at home.

Opportunities for Revenue Growth

The new intermediaries have used technology to create other revenue generating tools. There has always been distressed inventory, but networked technologies are allowing the industry to sell it effectively rather than let it perish. There has always been the aspirational non-user of hotel product and services. Now technology is allowing the industry to sell attractively packaged offerings to a market that heretofore has been difficult to identify and reach. Used intelligently, these businesses are adding a further arrow to the marketer's quiver - enabling the industry to add occupancy by targeting specific (and new) market segments. The extreme last-minute decision-maker and the highly price-sensitive traveller are both in this category.

Growing numbers of consumers now compare room facilities and rates, and they are learning to bid for rooms and spare seats on aircraft. A third-party can do the aggregation and the constant updating. It can also act as a brand buffer allowing companies to discount unsold seats or unsold rooms indirectly. Even with concerns about the competition, why let the value leak to the middleman?

The Internet's cost efficiency appeals to companies that currently manage travel offline, and it should lead to an increase in the number of companies that manage travel overall.We have seen the successful hotel businesses of the old economy partnering to compete with the start-up businesses of the new economy. As these ventures get off the ground, they have the potential to cut deeply into the revenue streams of the new Internet businesses, which have relied on commissions and on the sluggish response to market threats of the airlines and hotel companies. It will not be that easy to get companies with an ethos of confidentiality to cooperate with competitors - in the process promoting transparency to common customers. But by pooling their resources, the major hospitality and travel chains can develop portals quickly and at lower risk to compete in this dynamically changing market.

Corporate Travel

The corporate traveller is a key segment targeted by almost all the major brands. Corporate policy, rather than individual choice, increasingly dictates business travel. According to Forrester Research, Inc., companies eager to save travel and processing costs will mandate the use of Web-based corporate booking engines. The few remaining unmanaged business travellers will buy their business travel online as leisure bookers do.

Corporate policies will increasingly require travellers to use company-approved online booking engines. These engines deliver two elements to improved margins - directed use of a company's negotiated room rates with their preferred suppliers, as well as reduced service charges for making employee travel reservations. Due to the self-service nature of online business travel booking, companies and travel suppliers must increase efforts to encourage continued use.

The Internet's cost efficiency appeals to companies that currently manage travel offline, and it should lead to an increase in the number of companies that manage travel overall. Companies with larger travel budgets can be expected to be the first to shift their travel buying online with 70 percent of Fortune 1,000 companies making this migration by 2002, says Forrester. Larger accounts that are currently unmanaged will increasingly buy online and thus will soon adopt managed travel. Even smaller firms will move their business travel online as well, first encouraging individuals to use any Web interface, then gradually adopting targeted services.

Each managed traveller's company computer will include a desktop icon, which, after entering a user name and password, will link directly to a personalised profile within the travel site. Once business travellers sign on to corporate travel sites, entire trips can be booked with one click on the desktop icon, eliminating the need to re-enter login information. On the road, managed travellers will have the ability to research upcoming trips, check on late flights or change an existing hotel reservation.

Loyalty Challenge

Due to a combination of new bookers and the increasing amounts consumers are spending, the online travel market continues to boom. Travel sites, however, face the same challenges that online retailers struggle with - most consumers are not loyal. Web travellers rely upon the convenience, abundant information and low prices found online, and they are willing to research multiple sites for the best deals.

Forrester divides customers into three segments: disloyal, curious, and loyal bookers. "Disloyal" bookers, customers who research and book at multiple sites, search far and wide to find the best deals for their sophisticated travel needs - including the lowest prices, enticing special offers and exacting itinerary requirements. "Curious" bookers research multiple sites, yet return to the same site to book travel and accommodations. The third category identified by Forrester, "loyal" customers research and book at one site. Both curious and loyal consumers rely on one site due to easy site navigation, favourable previous experiences and low prices.

B2B applications are even bigger accelerators of change than those in the B2C space when it comes to how hospitality and travel companies will do business in the years ahead.Even though many customers aggressively seek choices to meet their needs, some sites attract more loyalty than others. The one-stop-shop nature of online travel agencies effectively attracts bookers that rely on one site for all their booking needs. Hotel chains, on the other hand, may have a harder time attracting loyal bookers because they are offering only one element of the travel package. Hotel chain web sites can lure disloyal bookers away from agency and consolidator web sites with special room rates and upgrade perks available exclusively online. Although portals have the greatest reach of all travel sites, they get the lowest percentage of bookers from all three segments.

To combat online booker disloyalty, hotels, agencies and portals must take lessons from online retailers on how to encourage loyalty. Suppliers must establish dynamic partnerships with suppliers in other travel categories that allow consumers to book flights, hotels, and car rentals at the same site. Hotel chains must sell adjacent categories of products and services. Portals should let the agencies and hotels fight over bookers and instead focus on what portals do best - offer information to consumers.

B2B Applications

B2B applications are even bigger accelerators of change than those in the B2C space when it comes to how hospitality and travel companies will do business in the years ahead. The B2B space is populated by many types of companies, including links among supply chain partners and market exchanges selling products and services online to businesses. eProcurement is one example of a growing B2B space in the hotel industry. Adoption of B2B strategies that connect businesses in varied ways is being driven by a number of factors:

Simplifying IT Infrastructures

Yesterday's information technology (IT) model was based on each hotel and/or hotel group maintaining an in-house IT team, which owned and managed the business's hardware and software. Tomorrow, most businesses will have migrated to an Application Service Provision (ASP) model. Under the ASP model, providers offer a variety of applications and services to companies, which these clients can access with nothing more than an Internet link to the ASP site. This marks a dramatic change from the traditionally defined "service bureau," which once involved the transmission of operational data to an outside agency for management by a remote application.

More recently, the explosion of Internet-based software applications and services by ASP providers has caused old economy and new economy businesses alike to revisit off-premises application processing. The processing of unit-level data at a distant site via an ASP provider may well represent one of the most important ways to obtain mission-critical IT solutions in the hotel industry on a cost-effective basis. Micros-Fidelio, for example, introduced the OPERA ASP application at HITEC. MICROS-Fidelio's Director of Hotel ASP Sales and Solutions, Barry Lowenthal, said: "The marketplace is moving toward seeing the value of ASP solutions. Some chains will do their own hosting, others want services provided."

Serious concerns remain about data ownership and the risk of whether the public Internet offers the speed, data security and reliability to support a highly interactive PMS application. But this is a dynamically changing area, and companies can expect to see ASP technology being introduced to radically simplify IT infrastructures. The ASP model will most likely be successful in the case of vendors offering a complete range of outsourced products - not just a PMS or CRS, but the complete systems operation for properties.

Mature businesses are not simply assuming that a focus on eBusiness is enough. The wireless market will introduce new competitive elements. Wireless Application Protocol (WAP) is a global specification that gives wireless devices - including mobile phones, personal digital assistants (PDAs) and computer terminals - access to the Internet. The distinguishing feature of wireless service is the ability to identify a user's location. The network seeks out the mobile phone to complete the call and knows where the holder of the phone actually is. This offers advertisers a dream channel to target customers in a personalised, time- and location-specific way. What are the potential applications or competitive threats?

Looking at the customer-facing systems, there is every likelihood that WAP-enabled functionality will be developed to provide access to hotel reservation systems and loyalty traveller databases. In the administrative areas, WAP technology can be applied to interface the mobile sales force with the centrally held customer relationship management (CRM) database - linking the revenue generating and cost generating systems in the bedroom (e.g. telephone, mini-bar, air-conditioning) to the centrally hosted property management system.

TECHNOLOGIES FOR DISASTER RECOVERY

Almost all hospitality companies have one main database for reservations and guest history. Both are at risk if a disaster occurs. In addition, the industry's reliance on technology and communication creates several less traditional risks. The global distribution system, the importance of customer data, productivity heavily reliant on terminals and information, and the long-term effect on loyalty of a single negative experience, are additional risks particularly present in the hospitality industry. In addition, companies are racing to build information about customer and spending patterns, investing millions of dollars in systems to institutionalize this knowledge. Loss of these systems and databases is analogous to organizational memory' loss. While rebuilding physical property may take several years, guest loyalty and behavioral history' may often require more time and money.

Clearly, the development of a technology disaster recovery' plan is an essential part of any company/s risk management programme. Its development and documentation at a minimum will require the following steps:

— *Take an Inventory* - Include items critical to the business, including the reservation system, database and the systems that support it. Telecommunications (dial-up lines, frame relay, dedicated lines and the Internet) can be included as support systems.

— *Assess Unavailability* - Assess what will occur if critical systems are absent over specific periods of time. Ask key questions for each system. What foreseeable impact exists if accounting functionality is down, for example, or the property management system applications are non-responsive? Determine the maximum amount of downtime for these critical items before there will be a significant impact on the business.

— *Identify Alternatives* - Identify disaster recovery alternatives for critical functions. Hospitality companies might decide that a "hot site" is a reasonable alternative with the loss of a reservation system. A hot site is a computer and data processing center with computers in place and waiting to be used by a company experiencing a disaster. Most hot sites are permanent facilities where the company can recreate its computing environment.

— *Determine Alternative Requirements* - Identify what is needed for an alternative to be implemented. Minimum requirements may involve telecommunications with certain bandwidths or dial-up lines. A specified level of power redundancy may be required for servers. Agreements with hardware vendors or vendors who provide disaster recovery sites may also be an option.

— *Identify Costs* - Gain an understanding of the total cost for each alternative. Examples of common costs include arranging hardware agreements with vendors or the cost of having a disaster recovery site available for use. Installation fees, purchase of redundant telecommunications, and the purchase of upgrading telecommunications (i.e., increasing bandwidth) are other common costs. Some hospitality companies may have additional costs relating to reservation system development time as a minimum alternative requirement.

— *Estimate the Recovery Period* - Estimate the amount of time until the critical systems become available. Each alternative should have a specified recovery period.

— *Define the Limitations* - Determine the limitations of each system back-up or alternative, including vendor agreements or hot sites. The plan needs to address questions of hardware replacement, especially if it is rare, discontinued, or a lag time exists between the purchase order and its delivery. The cost of an alternative or the length of time until availability may also be limitations.

— *Determine the Benefits* - Weigh the benefits of each alternative. Use the benefits of a faster recovery in the event of a disaster as a competitive advantage.

— *Test the Plan Annually* - Document the test and test results as a best practice to provide a record of any problems encountered and their resolution.

— *IT Training in Disaster Recovery* - Provide proper training of IT personnel for implementation of the disaster recovery plan.

When a disaster or hardware failure does occur, planning rigor will make all the difference in the speed of recovery. A completed disaster recovery plan for technology systems allows companies to realize large returns on a relatively small investment - minimizing what may otherwise be an unnecessary and costly outcome of disasters.

7

Advantages of E-distribution Systems

Key megatrends influencing the global hospitality industry in the new economy of the 21st century indicate that customer ownership will be the key to securing and maintaining competitive advantage. These megatrends, including consolidation, convergence, the cyclical nature of the industry, the efficient use of real estate, distribution systems, knowledge, outsourcing of non-core competencies, technology, and branding will have a profound influence on the day-to-day operations and long-term strategic direction in the hospitality and leisure industry in the coming decades.

Globalization is rapidly eliminating boundaries and borders; the rapid proliferation of technology is redefining the meaning of time and space as we know it. The result is the customer is empowered like never before. If the industry does not stay ahead of the curve and remain close to its customers, it faces the prospect of disintermediation as their service becomes increasingly commoditized through the proliferation of electronic commerce.Relationship management is the key to securing a stable customer base, but this is only possible through a deep understanding of customer needs and preferences.

Hospitality and leisure companies should invest in three key strategy areas.

CUSTOMER RELATIONSHIP MANAGEMENT

The business realities emerging with the New Economy drive the need for greater awareness in several aspects of customer ownership. To be successful and dynamic, leading edge hospitality companies will not give away markdowns unnecessarily, identify the most valuable customers, optimize promotions/advertising effectiveness via stealth one-to-one communication, ensure retention of valuable customers through targeted campaigns, and gain share-of-wallet by better understanding their customers.

KNOWLEDGE MANAGEMENT

Consistent with the drive to secure a greater share of the customer, the industry must actively seek ways to harness relevant knowledge from its guests, suppliers, employees and competitors. For the majority of hotels, ERP platforms currently in place are out of date and not integrated into customer data and guest satisfaction databases. There is also a need for the industry to begin to benchmark its performance in order to advance and evolve a universally recognized best practices operating standard.

OUTSOURCING NON-CORE COMPETENCIES

Increasingly, this is a key trend that extends beyond laundry and valet parking. A more significant area of operations is draining revenue from the bottom line – the finance and accounting function. Finance and accounting processes at the average hotel are running at more than two percent of revenue. This is more than double the best practice standards in a number of other industries. Less emphasis on non-critical functions will give hoteliers more time to focus on brand-building activities and satisfying their customers.

REDEFINING VALUE CHAIN FOR CONSUMERS

More than any other aspect of business, the Internet revolution is reshaping the concept of the value chain, and how goods and services are distributed to consumers. To grow and succeed, management at hospitality and travel companies of any size must juggle multiple distribution channels, customer segments and intermediaries in their distribution of goods and services. All entities have zeroed in on a business-to-consumer strategy with the intent to influence purchase decisions and own consumer loyalty.

Classic economic models place the producer of goods at one end of the chain and the consumer on the other end, with packaging, shipping, storing and retail middlemen often connecting the two. The Internet, however, has redefined the traditional model and all of the relationships within this value chain. Regardless of whether the good is a product, a service or a combination of the two, the entire consumer purchasing process is undergoing re-evaluation with new business models poised to change or destroy the traditional methods of distribution. Although the hospitality industry began to adopt electronic commerce some 30 years ago when the airline industry developed automated reservation systems, technology is causing massive redesign of product distribution and value creation.

The logical consequence of eDistribution is inescapable: the traditional value chain collapses in what can be described as a "frictionless environment," as suppliers interact directly with consumers through networked technologies. In a frictionless environment, when interaction costs at the margin are close to zero, the cost structure and strategic implications of distribution clearly change very significantly.

In the so-called "old economy," distribution intermediaries existed to compensate for the lack of knowledge on products and pricing, as well as bringing buyer and seller together over a physical distance. As the Internet becomes the ultimate connectivity tool, however, products and services no longer require a physical distribution presence. Intermediaries can continue to contribute to the product or service. But as technology forces out physical inefficiencies in distribution, there are fewer places where middlemen can find safe haven from disintermediation.

The implications of a collapse of the traditional value chain are immense. Because much of the hospitality travel product is experienced-based, the role of distribution can be seen at its simplest as the ability to initiate an experience.

Distribution, therefore, becomes part of the product itself. A redefined value chain has both positive and negative implications for each player in the chain. Generally speaking, suppliers benefit from lower distribution costs, better product image control, enhanced brand value and a better relationship with the customer. Intermediaries are likely to experience the greatest short-term turbulence, as each scrambles to assess the value they create and how to sustain it in the value chain. The consumer is most likely to gain, given the opportunity for better service, lower prices, tailored marketing and more options.

TRADITIONAL SUPPLIERS

Regardless of distribution method, the products themselves, such as physical guest rooms, airline seats and rental cars, remain largely unchanged in the new economy, although customer information can be used to customize products and services. What is markedly different, however, is an extraordinary increase in competitive pressure to "own" the customer. Since connectivity to the customer is no longer a technology hurdle, each player in the value chain is attempting to develop customer loyalty. Owning or, at a minimum, significantly influencing the channel is an important component of managing customer loyalty.

Numerous supplier limitations have allowed nimble start-ups to take an early lead in the race to influence the consumer purchase decision. Who would have suspected that initially Expedia.com would sell more inventory than the Web sites of some of its suppliers? Most legacy information technology (IT) systems have not been engineered to handle the volume, content and query capabilities required of an online presence in the distribution channel. Customer relationship management (CRM) systems, for example, remain largely in an infancy stage - only the top few percent of frequent hotel guests for example, receive consistent customized service.

Indeed, the vast majority of Web site screens do not mimic how consumers buy hospitality and travel products and services. To secure a hotel booking online, for example, the customer typically enters an arrival date and length of stay. In reality these variables often are influenced by price, but this symbiotic relationship is not well represented at Web sites. Web sites will clearly need to provide more information and suggestions for customized and packaged travel if they are truly to serve the interests of travelers. Consider the major issues for each of the key suppliers:

Airlines

The airlines have continued to be leaders in a shortening value chain by eliminating activities that do not add value, while developing such items as electronic ticketing and last-minute fares at low prices. Recently, five major airlines have announced they plan to create a megasite for eDistribution, a plan that responds to the threat of online travel agencies as they attempt to reintermediate themselves with customers. Whereas the airlines previously did not distribute their products directly to consumers, the new economy is requiring them to collaborate with their historical competitors with strategies to own the customer.

Hotel Companies

Channel conflict continues to be a significant issue among hotel companies. The price of a physical hotel room often varies widely depending on the source of booking. Even though "single-image" inventory is widely favored in the industry, displaying the same image to all potential buyers remains challenging and is largely unfulfilled. Legacy reservation systems were not designed for true single image inventory.

With available technology moving the industry toward price transparency, companies will feel intense pressure to compete on brand and differentiation, rather than price alone. Hotels must also manage additional customer touch points, an activity that is not always successful in the physical world. Guest recognition and tailored service are hallmarks of excellent properties.

Customer relationship management is powered by good data, however, which remains a rarity within the hotel community. Extending recognition and consistency of service to the Internet and new sales channels compounds the problem of effectively managing the entire guest experience.

Traditional Intermediaries

Changes brought by eDistribution have had the most profound effect on players that are positioned between suppliers and consumers in the distribution chain. These intermediaries are going through a period of transformation in how they do business:

Travel Agents

The retail travel agent is the best-known intermediary in the hospitality industry. A portion of a retailer's activities today remains value-added, while other roles are "old economy" in nature and becoming obsolete. The act of printing and issuing paper airline tickets is rooted in history when only Global Distribution System (GDS) terminals provided inventory access, and airlines required paper tickets for accounting. An area where travel agents do continue to add tremendous value is in advising travelers of destinations, tailoring travel to individual preferences, and saving time and money for the traveler before and during the trip. The new role for this group is that of knowledge manager.

Tour Operators

These intermediaries are also at significant risk from the collapse of the hospitality and travel value chain, as the Internet introduces new forms of competition. Tour operators aggregate travel products and repackage those products under a brand name. Tour operators in Europe own a much larger portion of the leisure travel market than in North America, with several large players dominating approximately half of the market.

In the United States and Canada, the tour business is extremely fragmented, with few well-known brands and thin profit margins. Suppliers connected with consumer groups have the potential to mimic and exceed the purchasing power of individual tour operators. What prevents well-branded airline, hotel, and car rental companies from agreeing to share inventory and creating their own packages? Nothing - as is the case with many packages offered today by airlines and hotel companies. Furthermore, customer loyalty is often stronger with the travel agent that sells packages in North America.

Immense business and technology issues also exist for tour operators seeking to function in the new economy. Call centers create an artificial demand regulator, limiting the amount of product available on a free-sale basis by the number of agents answering calls. If the same model and IT systems are opened to Web traffic, a virtually unlimited amount of demand could overwhelm free-sale and price-yielding techniques that are designed for a different business model. To compete, tour operators will need to use networking tools and offer complete excursions that are priced in real-time and tailored to their customers.

GDS and Switches GDS providers offer some of the most reliably engineered IT transaction systems in existence. In a frictionless environment, however, Internet connectivity could ultimately eliminate the need for the GDS. GDS providers are now powering many of the virtual travel agent and online supplier bookings, and are demonstrating that intermediaries can still play an effective role by delivering reservation capabilities faster and cheaper than individual suppliers on their own.

The fact that the GDS and switching organizations such as THISCO and Wizcom are still used to book online travel indicates that new entrants have eliminated only a part of the traditional hospitality and travel value chain. Some friction in distribution still exists when these intermediaries are used to gain access to supplier inventory.

New dot.com Intermediaries

Virtual travel agents represent a new form of intermediary, with some estimates placing the number of Web sites with travel booking capabilities at close to 1,000. Virtual travel agents charge a commission from suppliers, but typically offer a lower flat fee for airlines. Many of these companies will clearly have to revisit their Internet strategies and business models over the next several years, as hotels, airlines and other suppliers become more aggressive in offering consumers direct access to inventory. Many of these new dot.com companies have yet to be profitable and are running out of time and money to gain significant market share to offset high costs in technology and payroll.

New intermediaries such as Priceline.com have used the Internet to create a demand collection system. Worldres.com has amassed a central inventory of more than 11,000 properties, of which many are bed and breakfasts and vacation rentals that could not conform to the GDS listing requirements. A large number of additional entrants are expected in this arena in the next twelve months, particularly in the business-to-business arena, allowing corporations of all sizes to more effectively buy travel products.

Consumers

With the restructuring of the value chain, consumers stand to gain the most. Whether consumers choose to book online, or use the Internet for research and a physical travel agent to book, the level of knowledge, choices and convenience is unprecedented. The purchase experience will only improve as broadband access and multimedia content are married with product availability and one-to-one marketing activities. Distribution costs are eliminated when a value chain is shortened, and many of these savings are passed on to consumers in the form of bonus miles, last-minute fares and Web-direct-only pricing.

Vast amounts of information and the intensity of advertising "noise" can clearly be overwhelming to many consumers. But as the ease of use and customized offerings improve under the banner of powerful brands, the superiority of eBusiness applications for the hospitality and leisure industry will eventually become the norm. At that point, the new economy will no longer be "new," and the value chain will reflect the power of the Internet and its global networking capabilities.

ELECTRONIC SHELF SPACE

The hospitality business—and every other portion of its distribution chain, including suppliers, intermediaries and customers—is experiencing intense competition for the dissemination of information (including price and availability). The entire $200 billion travel and leisure industry worldwide has a stake in how travel information is distributed, and stands to gain or lose much in the emerging distribution model. As technologies continue to evolve, competing for the consumer purchase will increasingly take place in the virtual arena as players battle for "electronic shelf space."

As a result, the competition for electronic shelf space on the Global Distribution Network (GDN) is of critical importance in an industry where perception is reality and service is increasingly defined by technological advancements, rather than human interaction solely. The GDN is transforming the dynamics of the distribution environment -typified by the unrelenting clamor for the best position in the electronic market. As a result, travel and leisure industry companies must reevaluate their strategic positions in the distribution chain. Direct access to customers, the bread and butter of the existing value chain, remains at the forefront in terms of strategic direction.

Indeed, the electronic shelf space can be defined as the "real estate found on the computer screen. Almost all hospitality transactions taking place today, except for small country inns in Europe or the United States, employ some form of computer terminal where hotel availability is checked and reserved. For call center reservation agents, travel agents and individuals booking through the Internet, the physical screen, which displays GDN information, is the location of the virtual shelf space. Controlling electronic shelf space - and the number of "eyes" that view GDN information through one specific portal into this virtual inventory is of utmost importance to the world's leading hospitality and travel companies.

Emergence of GDN

At its inception, the Global Distribution System (GDS) represented a closed, dedicated connection of terminals displaying travel information about airlines, hotels, car rentals, cruises and other travel products. Used almost exclusively by travel agents, the GDS created a distribution chain that was relatively linear, allowing each chain player to collect a portion of the transaction. Today, however, the GDS has been reduced to just one component of a much larger ecosystem of networked travel information with advances in communication and software. It is this larger structure - the Global Distribution Network or GDN -that is dramatically affecting how business is done in the hospitality and travel industries. This emerging distribution model might be more closely described as a multi-dimensional flow of information and transactions - with any intermediary in the channel able to distribute travel information and complete a transaction directly with the customer.

Unlike many consumer products, which are displayed on physical store shelves, some degree of computerized inventory and distribution system is essential to display hospitality product information. Just as each supermarket aisle displays individual, physical items, specific domains and locations in electronic commerce house hospitality information. GDS providers, such as Galileo, Apollo, Worldspan or Sabre, often represent these domains. Increasingly, however, Internet-based travel companies, on-line access providers and other virtual communities appeal directly to consumers and travel agents, thereby circumventing the traditional GDS.

As a result, hospitality and travel suppliers must develop comprehensive channel management strategies to maximize yield for each existing channel and new component. In addition to the existing GDS, online access providers, Internet service providers, virtual communities, emerging intermediaries and direct connectivity among different suppliers must all be considered and evaluated separately as part of a channel management strategy.

Traditionally, the electronic shelf space was found in two places: either the travel agent's desktop or at the reservation center of individual suppliers (accessed by consumers via the telephone). The airline or hotel supplier was connected to travel agents through the GDS, which created a straightforward variable cost structure to sell travel products. Although designed for the airlines, the GDS's widespread distribution (currently 40,000 terminals worldwide) attracted other hospitality and travel companies to list their inventory.

Since their information is displayed in a similar format to airlines, hotel, car rental and tour wholesaler products are compromised on the GDS because of limited description and display of information, as well as the inability to sell inventory directly from a central reservation system. The inventory is essentially on consignment to the GDS at a pre-determined price, regardless of market fluctuations after the product allotment was made available. The end-consumer, travel agents and suppliers had two forms of communication the GDS terminal or the telephone.

With the evolution of the Internet, however, the shelf space has grown exponentially and become much more complex. In fact, the electronic shelf space is now quite crowded. Many suppliers (hotel, airline, and car rental companies) tour and travel companies, virtual agents and travel agents maintain web sites and conduct business over the Internet. In addition, some web sites offer various levels of travel information and advice, most of which are linked to one or more of the above booking engines. Combined, these groups are expected to account for $2 billion in bookings annually by the year 2002~~ All of these entities are targeting the computer screen through which consumers and travel agents view the world. Each entity exerts influence on one or more channels in the distribution model.

Channel Management

Channel management for hospitality and travel companies requires more than simply understanding the value chain and managing the players. Hospitality companies will need to develop business measurements that effectively represent digital commerce, determining the health and profitability of each available channel. Effective information auditing and analysis will become standard in each organization's sales strategy. Tools such as decision-support systems. data warehousing, and On Line Analytical Process (OLAP) systems will be required to respond to the market dynamics of each channel and its customers.

Completing a customer-initiated transaction includes product maintenance. information inquiries, inventory access and technical infrastructure to support these distribution developments. Indeed, Jupiter Communications, a new media research firm helping companies make business decisions about consumer interactivity, believes the largest opportunity for sellers of complex travel products - such as cruises and rooms at resorts - lies in integrating the online channel into existing sales channels to reduce the sales cost. Integrated sales channels will help travel companies qualify customers online, reducing the number of calls to close sales of higher-priced products off-line.

Technology by itself does not provide the solution, however. The creative integration and use of today's emerging channel network provides the potential for successful distribution management. Each travel supplier is required to carefully thread each customer through the most effective channel.

Requiring excellent coordination between any intermediary and supplier, the functional success to the customer is measured by accurate and timely information on an electronic shelf that owns the greatest amount of computer screen real estate.

Players

The hospitality and travel players battling for electronic shelf space can be found in three major categories Suppliers, Intermediaries and Customers. Suppliers contract to provide travel information in various channels for a fee. Channel providers pass the travel information onto the customers and seek to motivate certain customers to use their channel with incentive fees. Individual customers might receive incentive fees from the channel provider and commissions from the supplier.

Each player has its own set of challenges for management. Past business strategies do not apply to the GDN. The virtual communities of the GDN have unique business requirements as they are created with players clustering around themes or connected interests. It is these virtual communities that form the "neighborhoods" where customers tend to congregate. Each cluster is focused on information services, products, customer demographics or new business models that take advantage of the new technologies. Tactics for building the customer relationship include developing virtual communities from strategic alliances between companies such as America Online and Preview Travel. Strategic alliances such as these are creating more attractive virtual communities by providing an appealing product and services. Customer participation is a very important characteristic in virtual communities because it is the one factor that differentiates this model from other markets. The behavior of travel agents on the GDS and customers who are currently buying products and services online clearly indicate that companies can increase the volume of transactions in their digital channels. Companies have the opportunity to increase service levels, provide personalized interaction that builds customer loyalty, and provide new services that have been previously unavailable. Companies that understand the GDN will benefit from these valuable resources.

Suppliers

Players in the travel supply arena include airlines, hotels, rental car companies and tour and travel wholesalers involved in the provision of air, lodging, tours, car hire and destination services for travelers. The challenge for suppliers will be to manage and control the multiple entities that make up their GDN. Companies that participate in virtual communities must be willing to relinquish portions of inventory control and capacity management. Existing yield management techniques will need to be adapted to allow companies to effectively participate in the GDN. The rate at which distribution channels are changing is alarming.

Suppliers will be challenged to determine the level of integrating the GDN into their organization. Suppliers in general seem to lack a vision of where the GDN market is going and the role technology is playing in determining the future of the travel industry. In addition, the high cost of distribution is now causing many suppliers to reevaluate current distribution strategies. Southwest Airlines, for example, has chosen Sabre as its sole global distribution system for low-cost distribution. In addition, it created a robust interactive Internet site that had booking capabilities. A secondary effect of streamlining and lower cost was increased demand for Southwest products.

Intermediaries

These companies include internet providers, Telephony/ Call Centers (Worldwide toll-free numbers automatic call detection systems, GDS marketing media solutions) and Universal Switch Providers. These switches are communications devices that translate, convert and exchange information between hotel systems (CRS's or PMS's and airline GDS's). Universal switches assist the travel supplier by providing suppliers with "one-stop shopping" for equal access to the assorted GDS providers. The hotel supplier currently is the only beneficiary of switch providers. Numerous opportunities exist for additional universal switch players for hotel as well as other travel suppliers.

Currently there are two providers for hotel universal switches: Pegasus Systems' THISCO and Cendant's WizCom. Select hotels have integrated the switches into a distribution strategy to provide universal access from their Property Management Systems (PMS) and Central Reservations System (CRS) to the GDS's, and the Internet. Suppliers that go direct to the customer represent an obvious threat to intermediaries. Any player in the value chain can pirate a customer from an intermediary in the GDN. Channel providers have the potential to leverage strong existing virtual communities by adding new products and services to the value chain immediately. Travel suppliers that create direct links to customers will be able to chip away from intermediaries.

Customers

Entities with direct access to customers include travel agents, online travel agents, Internet/online service providers, corporate travel departments, company representatives that coordinate travel for employees, and individual travelers or agents acting on behalf of the consuming traveler. Clearly, the role of travel agents has evolved rapidly as they seek to remain competitive given the growth of the electronic shelf space. In simple terms, travel agents no longer serve as order-takers holding the monopoly on GDS access. In the new distribution model, travel agents become knowledge brokers, serving as travel consultants who add validity and credibility to the information.

Building Presence on Electronic Shelf Space

Hospitality companies must place their product on the best electronic shelf to maximize their exposure. and share of the customer. The traditional adage of "location, location location" in the hotel business rings especially true within the GDN. Corporate success within the GDN is determined largely by location in the electronic arena. The most desirable "shelf space" location resides in specific virtual portals, such as browsers (United Airlines, America Online, Netscape, Microsoft Internet Explorer), on-line communities, the alliances dictating travel information, interlinks (electronic advertising, web site links, and other) and the intermediaries that represent the branded travel product to a company's key target audience.

Hospitality companies will benefit as they conduct feasibility studies investigating how to build presence on an electronic shelf space and determining which distribution channel to select. Key questions must be answered. What is the best market mix on the GDN? Who are the target customers, and what areas of the GDN are predominately used by which customers? Given that traditional call center reservations can be six times as costly as electronic ones, what channels are most cost effective? What are the saving benefits and increased risks of an expanded GDN presence? In what ways must information be managed as it flows back, and how does that enable direct one-to-one marketing? Ultimately, a company must achieve two goals:

— Allow customers to search for products and services they are willing to purchase;

— Provide a means to fulfill the transaction immediately.

Channel performance and management is critical at the first stage, and involves multiple decisions. Bundling services is also essential in providing one-stop shopping. In the virtual community, linking multiple suppliers, destinations, and products is effortless when compared to a physical one-stop shopping center. Customers are eager to access all information with as few clicks as possible, whether they are travel agents, corporate travel planners or end consumers. And finding which customers are most profitable becomes an additional task of effective channel management. Virtual communities are much like physical ones, with large differences in interests, incomes and demographics. Controlling the largest channel is not always the best business strategy. While one channel may include millions of online users, selling specific leisure destinations may require a more refined and niche virtual community to target.

HOSPITALITY EPROCUREMENT

The hospitality industry has historically struggled under the weight of fragmented supply chains, made even more unwieldy by complex and inefficient business processes in distribution and procurement. Now that fragmentation may be put right as old economy hospitality companies turn to eBusiness startups to move procurement and distribution processes online. In short, eProcurement offers the potential for improving both ends of the equation to reduce costs, generate new revenue streams and improve audit control.

Growth in hospitality eProcurement is clearly explosive in its potential, and our view is that hotel organizations will need to respond to this new market to remain competitive. Nevertheless, there are major obstacles to the industry seizing the advantages of eProcurement and realizing improvements in the supply chain.

The Internet's ability to deliver information in a common format to a wide array of computers enables businesses to access and share information from many sources - including their customers, financial institutions and suppliers. eProcurement is a direct outgrowth of that capability. As a global network using standardized protocols and universal connectivity, the Internet opens the door for businesses to develop international marketplaces for their products and services.

Not only does the Internet facilitate the sharing of information, it simplifies the process for the end-user as well, and reduces infrastructure and transaction costs. The shared nature of the Internet distributes the infrastructure costs across large groups of potential customers, suppliers and others. That means businesses of any size can gain access for a variety of purposes. Distributors or suppliers can build revenue while also realizing reduced customer contact costs. Rather than maintaining multiple sales contact systems, suppliers need to have just one connection to the Internet.

What is the real potential for hospitality companies? eProcurement will have a positive impact on business functions and processes for those organizations that fully take advantage of these capabilities. Buyers, for example, have a growing amount of information available to identify the suppliers with whom they want to do business. eProcurement facilitates the aggregation of small purchases, thereby making the order process more efficient and cost effective. And it minimizes the need for intermediaries between the supplier and buyer. Traditional supply chain distributors, as a result, are being forced to provide value-added services to remain viable in the chain.

We begin by defining eProcurement. Using digitized processes, the procurement process is engineered in concert with an all-electronic design and implementation of the infrastructure required to source, supply, manage and control services. It is one of the most important of business-to-business (B2B) functions.

eProcurement solutions were initially launched by companies such as Ariba, Inc., which developed corporate procurement systems for global 2000 companies to give their employees access to vendors electronically. Though effective, these applications centering on "buy-side" solutions were inherently expensive and time-consuming to implement. The new generation of eProcurement is more revolutionary. Today, digital marketplaces create Internet portals to serve multiple buyers and sellers in the exchange of goods and services. These new ventures are leveling the playing field for both buyers and suppliers, giving smaller companies and those around the world ready access, using a Web browser, to opportunities once available primarily to larger companies in North America. Large up-front investments in hardware and software are unnecessary. To draw traffic to portals, some providers - including Vertical Net, hglobe.com and hospitalitynet.org - have bundled targeted content, career services and discussion forums along with procurement services.

Emerging Marketplace Models

To participate in the development of eProcurement offerings, hospitality companies will benefit by understanding the emerging digital marketplace models. There are currently two dominant models:

Industry-specific marketplaces

Organizations with domain expertise in a particular industry - or industry "vertical" in the language of the new economy - launch these exchanges. These market-places support commerce specific to an industry as they seek to aggregate buyers and sellers to reduce transaction costs. Their competitive advantage is based on a unique understanding of industry inefficiencies. Examples can be seen in Marriott International's and Hyatt's P-Co - a joint, independent electronic purchasing network powered by GoCo-op's eCommerce engine - that leverages economies of scale to reduce prices on product and services. Or consider Instill Corporation, which links food service operators and food service product distributors/ manufacturers. Instill bundles eProcurement services to improve control and management of foodservice purchasing, offers a consolidated purchase information service for monitoring contract compliance and capturing rebates, provides market intelligence to manufacturers, and creates an online community and marketplace for small chains and independent operators to improve their operating and financial performance.

Horizontal marketplaces

These exchanges provide a vehicle for many types of buyers and sellers to advertise, share content, bid on products, participate in auctions and manage their supply chains. Such marketplace sites serve a wide range of disparate industries and/or provide them with access to horizontal applications.

Unlike the original eProcurement systems, which generally provided static catalogs and limited sourcing capability, these new digital marketplaces use dynamic pricing models - primarily auctions or exchanges - which are based on demand. Additionally, some marketplaces, such as those powered by Zoho.com, can interface with companies' enterprise resource planning (ERP) and accounting systems.

Horizontal marketplaces have multiple revenue streams, the most common of which come from advertising on sites. Many of these marketplaces also generate revenues in the form of commissions charged to sellers participating in auctions. Storefront sales to sellers can be an additional source of revenue for such marketplaces. Tradeout.com, one such example of a horizontal marketplace, categorizes its services to multiple industries by product type. Its services include the hosting of seller–driven auctions for excess inventory resale. In such auctions, sellers list their products and receive price bids from multiple buyers for individual products, thereby enabling the seller to potentially receive the highest price for their products, including any excess inventory that ordinarily would have to be written off. Vertical marketplaces have similar revenue sources, although they are able to command higher advertising fees due to the detailed information they can collect on concentrated groups of members and subscribers.

Additionally, some of them also generate revenues by charging subscription fees to access their focused content and product data.

In contrast to vertical marketplaces, horizontal marketplaces face challenges specific to their broad mission. Based on the need to appeal to diverse industries, these marketplaces must satisfy the product, service and content needs of their varied buyers and members, and may be fighting an uphill battle in doing so. Some companies have been successful using this model, but they have had to invest in expensive domain experts to develop the compelling offerings typically available in a vertical marketplace. The diversity of the industries served by horizontal marketplaces, however, can be useful in reducing risk in the event of limited penetration in a particular vertical.

A hybrid marketplace model is beginning to emerge with the advantage of leveraging the strengths of both models. In this model several contiguous verticals are represented in a marketplace. These contiguous verticals can be grouped according to the similar products and services used by all, yet still maintain the content and other offerings unique to each.

A hybrid market–place, for example, might provide an exchange for food service, hospitality and grocery industry members, such as VerticalNet's e-hospitality.com, which could be grouped together to access food and beverage suppliers. In contrast, hospitality industry member sites might feature only FF&E items, such as beds. Buyers can benefit from hybrid models of digital marketplaces because they can potentially access more sellers and therefore have more bargaining power.

Implications of eProcurement

eProcurement clearly offers significant opportunities for hospitality industry players to improve their supply chains, and those companies that ignore the potential may suffer in the long run. During these early stages of the eProcurement revolution, relationships among buyers, sellers and competitors will be redefined. Additionally, global eBusiness will be fueled by the ability to track the movement of trade goods at any point along the supply chain. Ships transporting goods from Latin America to North America, for example, might be quickly redirected to Europe in the event that bids were greater in other locations. Such flexibility in real-time pricing would greatly minimize reliance on fixed prices.

We can summarize the implications for various segments of the hospitality industry in the following points:

Brand parents

— Established brands can leverage their relationships, experience, knowledge and purchasing power to reengineer corporate purchasing efforts for improved efficiency.

— These players can develop (or partner with vendors and/or with competitors) private, secure, customized sites for employees to purchase products and services from approved vendors. Real-time inventory management and accounting then becomes possible.

— The major brands can also take control of the procurement process by minimizing "maverick" purchases and monitoring adherence to approved vendor lists, ensuring their employees adhere to quality standards.

Management companies and independents

— These companies will gain access to rebates traditionally only available to larger companies based on aggregated demand.

— The buying power of hotels outside North America, which have had little clout historically, should be increased.

— Management will be able to leverage public access applications that provide access to extensive vendor networks and their products in horizontal or vertical marketplaces.

— Moving processes online should result in labor cost savings.

Future Trends

To fully leverage the benefits of end-to-end eProcurement, hospitality companies need to position procurement more strategically and demand value-added services from providers to manage the entire supply chain from requisition to payment. Customer care services - a critical component of these solutions - must be situated throughout the supply chain to enable hospitality companies to realize the full benefits.

Market forces are promoting marketplaces that encompass several contiguous verticals, rather than a single vertical focus of products or services. In hybrid market-place exchanges, managers of individual verticals will continue to need a great deal of domain expertise. However, they will also be able to cross-pollinate and leverage the capabilities of other market-places to benefit each one of their industries individually. This will promote eProcurement offerings that are moving toward one-stop shopping, while providing vertical-specific services. In the medium-term we anticipate that eBusiness ecosystems will emerge as the next wave of eProcurement solutions. These interconnected worlds will allow organizations (employees, suppliers and customers) to transact via a single point for commerce and information, creating a global web of digital markets and corporate exchanges. This new wave of development will provide hospitality companies with clear benefits:

— Competitive and dynamic pricing.

— Ability to customize marketplaces. This will result in minimized searching costs through vendor-specific interfaces to facilitate adherence to quality standards and vendor comparison.

— Consolidated reporting and accounting to monitor supply chain performance and improve budgeting.

— Single point of contact for customer care.

— Access to international distribution networks.

— Process improvements in handling purchase orders.

— Customized online order-flow-tracking capability that is based on a company's internal workflow routing process.

— Streamlined buyer and supplier commerce processes.

— Shared network of commerce services.

— New methods of dynamic sourcing and trade.

— Extended customer reach and enhanced customer service.

— Meaningful tools to facilitate marketplace interaction.

To fully leverage the benefits of end-to-end eProcurement, hospitality companies need to position procurement, hospitality companies need to position procurement more strategically and demand value-added services from providers to manage the entire supply chain from requisition to payment.

8
Hotel Profit Management

An issue developing within the lodging industry is whether or not Profit Per Available Room (ProfPAR) is a better way to measure hotel performance than the well-known Revenue Per Available Room (RevPAR) statistic. Specifically, the main question is – Does RevPAR miss some important economic phenomena that ProfPAR reveals? Arguably, the first steps in gaining insight about the ProfPAR vs. RevPAR debate are to clarify the definition and measurement of profit and to obtain a better understanding of how historical revenue and profit movements differ.

Profit may be defined in many ways to address particular business topics. Operating profit from hotels represents the operating decisions made by an owner, or in many cases the management team employed by the owner. As a result, operating profits show how successful managers have been in generating income from property operations. RevPAR however, only reflects rooms revenue, which is heavily influenced by factors managers cannot control, such as business travel and the general economy.

The following definitions of profit measures are used:
— Operating Profit = Total Revenue – Total Operating Expenses.

Total operating expenses include management fees, insurance, and property taxes, but do not include interest, rent, depreciation & amortization, and capital reserve.

— Operating Profit Margin = Operating Profit/Total Revenue.

The operating profit margin quantifies operating decisions and shows how well managers have produced income from different levels of revenue over time.

— ProfPAR = Operating Profit per Year/Daily Available Rooms per Year.

To provide historical perspective on operating profit, we use three samples from Trends in the Hotel Industry survey, which has been conducted annually for close to 70 years. We examined total revenues, total operating expenses, operating profit, and the operating profit margin for an all-hotel sample, full-service hotels, and limited-service properties. The data in the three samples reflect the average unit-level, dollars per-available room of hotels for which we have 20 years of comprehensive information.

When examining the all-hotels sample, revenues increased over time, with operating expenses logically following due to the variable nature of expenses in the hotel business. However, the gap between revenue and operating expenses is the not constant beginning in the early 1990s. This gap represents operating profit, and the larger and more sustained the gap, the more unit-level managers have controlled operating expenses regardless of total revenue. The profit margin line simply translates the operating profit dollars per available room to the percentage of total revenues that falls to operating profit.

The operating profit margin for all-hotels has trended upward since 1991, and peaked at 32.9% in 2000, meaning that almost 33% of the total revenue of a property went straight to the bottom-line. The 2002 operating profit margin is estimated to be 28.1%, which is higher than the operating profit margin generated in 14 of the 20 years studied. This indicates that while we know RevPAR has been declining at rates not seen over the past 15 years, managers have effectively handled operational expenses.

The sample of full-service hotels shows a similar pattern to that of the all-hotels sample. Revenue increases are followed closely by operating expense increases until the early 1990s, when the gap widens and operating profit increases. The operating profit margin for full-service hotels peaked in 2000 at 30.6% and registered an estimated 25.7% in 2002, one of the more operationally challenging years in the past two decades.

Limited-service hotels also show an increasing operating profit over time as the gap between total revenue and total operating expenses has widened. The operating profit margin for limited-service properties peaked in 1997 at 42.6% and registered an estimated 35.6% in 2002.

High operating profits and profit margins can mean two things: sales are increasing faster than expenses or operating costs are controlled effectively. Based on the data examined by HRG, it appears that both of these explanations apply to the average hotel in each sample. Revenue began to increase in the 1990s and expenses followed at a lower growth rate. However, this discrepancy in revenue and expense growth rates was sustained over a decade, indicating that managers have been effectively controlling costs since the early to mid-1990s.

YIELD MANAGEMENT SYSTEM MEASUREMENT

The hotelier plots daily revenues from the past several years, and searches his or her findings for any type of trends. Spikes from the statistical noise produced from seasonality and demand fluctuations are smoothed to determine stable patterns. The patterns are used as a basis for making future projections, which are expected to grow at a steady rate. By comparing the future projections with any deviation from the projections, the amount of deviation, in theory, may be tied to the system. However, this approach fails to account for the impact of new events that happened after the system was installed - new marketing campaigns or the introduction of a web site, for example - which were not done in the past. It still makes it impossible to see what revenue change is due to the system or to other factors.

A process is used to estimate what the unconstrained demand would have been or may have been. The process considers demand "on the books" and, after there is no more hotel capacity, it attempts to figure the amount of demand turned down. With this information in hand, the hotelier speculates that, if he or she accepted the best business mix after the fact, how much revenue would have the property generated. That amount is compared to the actual amount of revenues. This difference or "gap" offers a possible measure for improvement. The "gap" before the system install is weighed against the "gap" after the system installation. The difference perhaps illustrates the system's impact. Simply, this approach only teaches the hotelier how to be wiser after the event, instead of making the best decisions for future booking opportunities. If you made investment decisions, in the stock market, for example, solely after the fact, knowing how prices fluctuated, and realizing when would have been the best time to buy and sell, you still would not enjoy optimum return because the decisions did not factor future volatility and uncertainty. This approach can not separate what the system is doing and what is being affected by changing market conditions and other factors.

In an attempt to estimate the yield management system results, revenues from a period after system installation are compared to a similar period last year prior to installation. To consider the effect of extraneous factors on revenues, the comparison is tracked against any demand fluctuations from a similar hotel (without the yield management system) in the same competitive set, and/or with nearly the same demographics.

Hotels and resorts pride themselves in their uniqueness. So it is impossible to imagine two hotels that would experience identical affects from the extraneous factors, and it is highly unlikely they would share the same pricing strategies directed or the same marketing mixes.

It is vital that the system measurement is conducted in such a manner as to isolate the changes in market conditions and the business environment. One of the first places where this type of system measurement with isolation was attempted was in a controlled environment, using computer simulation.

In this case, a yield management practice with basic demand data is deployed. First, booking decisions from the yield management practice are based on simulated human decisions, which result in bookings accepted and not accepted.

Next, the booking decisions are based on yield management system decisions. Again, bookings are accepted and not accepted.

Accepted bookings from both decision scenarios translate into revenue, and the compared revenues between the two illustrate how the yield management practice may deliver results. However, how can computer simulation understand truly how the humans would have acted? Humans are not efficient at executing on "first come and first served." Even if the measurement shows benefits in a controlled environment, how can the hotelier be assured that there will be benefits in the "real" world.

If demand does increase due to marketing programmes or an improvement in economy after the yield system installation, occupancy will increase, and there will be more sold-out nights. But what if there is no increase in demand compared to last year, while an effective yield management practice is put into place? As a result of the yield management system, it is anticipated that there will be a reduction in the number of turn downs multi-night stays. And the proper overbooking of rooms leads to a decrease in the amount of empty rooms on sold-out nights.

Thus, occupancy will increase through the better yield practice. The scientific measurement approach is the tool with which it can be precisely determined whether the occupancy increased because of the yield management practice or due to marketing programmes or improved economic conditions. It begins by identifying periods where the system does not restrict the hotel or resort in accepting bookings. This starts the process by which a look at what is occurring in the marketplace and in the local economy is gained. Scientific measurement isolates the impact of the marketing programmes and economic factors from the impact of the yield management solution. It shows what room revenue increases can be attributed to the yield management solution.

LEVERAGING THE REAL VALUES

The hospitality industry has historically measured itself with a standard metric used worldwide - revenue-per-available-room (REVPAR). More than simply a way to quantify results, REVPAR reflects our industry's fundamental structure and value proposition based on physical assets (hotel rooms) as the driver of wealth. With the magnitude of change driven by technology, it is now essential to ask is REVPAR still the best measure of performance for a hotel organization, or does it reflect an outmoded view of a hotel's performance horizon? We submit that the latter is the case. Technology is changing every aspect of how we live, work and profit, and it should come as no surprise that technology must also change how the hospitality industry serves customers and measures itself. In short, the "end game" can no longer be REVPAR - revenue measured by the physical asset.

The most profitable hotel organizations of the future will be those that capture an increasing share of the customer's purchasing power - while they are in the hotel, at home or anywhere else in the world. What drives this change is technology, which makes it possible to serve customers in both physical place (the hotel room) and virtual space (anytime and anywhere). The historic measure of hotel performance - REVPAR - must thus give way to a metric that reflects the customer as the more fundamental driver of value in the hospitality industry. Revenue-per-available-customer (REVPAC) does just that.

Today, hotel organizations are no longer constrained by physical location in serving customers. New media and systems technologies offer extraordinary efficiencies in delivering products and services with greater speed, lower cost and improved flexibility. Furthermore, technology offers unprecedented opportunities for innovation in an industry's changing menu of products and services. What does this mean for our industry? We are witnessing a period of major change as the fundamental value proposition of our industry is overturned. Customers - not physical assets - drive wealth in all industries, and the hospitality industry is certainly no exception. Technology deployed in enterprise-wide platforms makes it possible to get closer to customers. It provides tangible benefits as it offers opportunities to increase business value, reduce operational costs and create new opportunities for growth in the industry.

Technology is fundamentally changing the banking industry and has become not merely a way to boost productivity but an important - and profitable -channel for delivering (new and additional) financial services." 'That is just as true for hospitality, as it is in other industries.At stake is technology's impact on customer equity - defined as the degree to which an industry has fully developed relationships with its customers, providing them with more products and services to meet exiting and emerging needs. REVPAC, as a measure of performance, embodies a shift in perspective from an "asset play" based on hotel properties and rooms to a focus on leveraging customer equity for shareholder wealth.

REVPAC casts a spotlight on a number of key questions for the industry on the eve of the 21st century. How can hotel organizations "talk" to customers in a way they have never been spoken to before by the industry? What must companies do to "hear" their customers in new ways, learning how to better represent them and their needs in the market? How can hospitality organizations maximize revenues by making the most of their relationships with customers? Hotel guests are not lust customers who seek room and board, and perhaps a fax machine in the room. They represent a consumer with an array of needs, whose time is Limited and who, in many cases, will respond to diverse products, improved service and convenience.

In the future, the traditional "marketplace" will be greatly expanded to incorporate the virtual environment or "marketspace" - a market context and environment rendered accessible by technology as physical location becomes irrelevant. Understanding the potential of both the marketplace and marketspace sets the stage for delivery of expanded products and services - some traditional, others less so - to customers.

Technology thus plays a key role, both in delivering products and service in virtual space, but also in enhancing the ability to listen and talk with customers in new ways. Sophisticated management information systems allow companies to identify with increasing precision the customer segments and markets that offer the greatest opportunities for growth, given the pace of change in a global economy. A technology platform must incorporate two systems, however, to support the hospitality industry's potential for improving customer equity. Customer reservations systems track *when* and *where* customers are going, and *what* they will do when they get there. Customer information systems track *who* the customers are, *what* they purchase, and *how* they live and work. Hospitality companies already use reservation systems to get customers into the hotel. Information systems generate customer profiles based on tracking consumption patterns in the process defining a diverse range of wants and needs.

This poses a number of challenges. Certainly, it will be important to integrate data generated at the property level with reservations systems and customer information in a total system solution that provides for data warehouses and networked communications. In such a system, customer information is captured from a variety of sources, and becomes the platform for the highly focused marketing and product development strategies of the future.

The hospitality in the industry will thus require two types of infrastructure to do business - real estate and technology - to support a shirt from depending on "place" to a reliance on "space" to fully meet customer needs. This follows a four-stage evolution currently taking place in industries across the board.

The hospitality industry, for example, historically focused on developing major physical assets, with an almost exclusive orientation to financing and building individual properties. At this first stage, companies achieved relatively low customer equity, providing a narrow band of products and services, traditional to the hospitality industry, at various physical locations. As the industry matured, it differentiated itself to meet more diverse customer needs with properties matched to the various market niches. In this second stage, business hotels and all-suite properties are examples of such differentiation. A third stage involves serving customers in ways that do not require a physical address at all, including telephone marketing and catalog sales. And in the fourth state - the age of electronic commerce - the "real estate" is actually owned by the consumers themselves in the form of a personal computer located on a desktop, eliminating the need for many types of businesses to own significant physical assets in order to create wealth.

At each of these stages, the potential for customer equity rises with increased access to customers, regardless of their physical location, while the costs associated with fixed-assets (real estate) declines. The evolutionary track moves from exclusive reliance on major assets to combinations of physical assets and technology in reaching customers. Indeed, new media and systems technologies can be designed to give hotel organizations greatly enhanced access to larger numbers of customers - regardless of physical location. These technology platforms also spawn rapid innovation in products and services, combined with improved speed to market. The result enhanced business valuation and higher stock prices as a company's strategic, technological and financial architectures are aligned to generate customer equity.

Hospitality companies can dramatically improve the valuation of their companies by using new technology to bring them closer to their customers. This is particularly the case with major companies that have not fully served their large customer bases and have good potential to build customer equity. In many cases these organizations are our industry's major franchisors, whose goals are typically to sign up new franchisees and improve the yields from each property. In a nutshell, these companies are using franchising as a growth vehicle and their orientation is to maximizing fee income.

For these organizations, an intermediate performance measure might be described as revenue-per-available-franchisee (REVPAF). The challenge here will be to develop ways to reach the primary customer (hotel guest) directly, rather than simply through the franchisee organizations - with the end game being improved REVPAC. The typical franchisor catches the primary customer in its reservation system, but typically doesn't "speak" to that customer again, either during the guest stay or after leaving the hotel property. Franchisors will benefit as they begin to develop the strategies and systems allowing them direct access to the primary customers, with a goal of increasing REVPAC.

VALUE VOLATILITY

When we think of the term "value" of a hotel we traditionally think of "appraised or market" value. It is important to keep in mind, however, that there are different approaches to appraisal value i.e. the replacement cost, comparable sales and the capitalization of income or discounted cash flow approach to value. And in today's environment, these different approaches can potentially yield very different "values" depending upon the particular situation and certain key assumptions.

In addition to "appraised" value, there are also the concepts of "Highest and Best Use" Value ", "NAV or Net Asset Value", "Assessed Value", "Investment Value" and "Liquidation value" that potentially need to be understood and reconciled as well.

Hotel values can fluctuate due to many factors including the following:

— Changes in the net income generated from the hotel
— changes in the value of underlying real estate
— changes in investment risk versus return expectations (cap rates /discount factors) and/or
— changes in the availability/cost of capital.

And it is very important to understand how each of these factors alone and in combination potentially impact the value of a particular hotel.

While there are potential "sellers" and clearly also potential "buyers" for hotels, during these past several months there have been very few transactions. And this is due primarily to a significant gap between what buyers are willing to pay for a hotel and what sellers are willing to sell a hotel for, or often referred to as "ask" versus "bid" terms.

Many are asking why the reluctance of sellers to sell and what is different about today versus 10 years ago when many hotels ended up selling at deeply discounted prices.

There are two circumstances in particular which have changed dramatically which are influencing today's buy and sell decisions. One is the ability of the industry to absorb cash flow shortfalls and the other is alternative investment performance.

Ability to absorb cash flow shortfalls – today the industry is much better positioned to "weather the cash flow shortfall" storm. In 1990, the worst performance year ever for the hotel industry, the industry reported a loss of $5.4 billion and it was estimated at the time that over 40% of hotels were not covering debt service and as many as 80% of all hotels were generating little or not return on investment. Many hotel owners had no choice but to sell.

Alternative investment performance – ten years ago the hotel industry was reporting negative returns and at the time an investor could potentially earn a higher return from a certificate of deposit investment with minimal or no risk.

Changes in the terms and availability of debt capital can impact the value of a hotel. And changes in cap rates also impact hotel values. In today's environment, however, it is differences in thinking between buyers and sellers about the net income stream for a hotel that appears to account for much of the disconnect in ask vs bid terms and expectations.

— *From the sellers perspective.* During recent months many potential sellers have absorbed significant financial shortfalls from the fallout of the events of September 11th and the economy.

— *And buyers.* In light of recent events are understandably reluctant to pay for or give "value" credit for projected or forecasted improvement in the cash flow performance of a hotel.

Hotels that can demonstrate that they can rebuild business will be able to restore value, hotels expected to face on-going challenges rebuilding business will most likely experience declines or erosion in value.

It is important to keep in mind that individual hotel performance can vary dramatically from the industry as a whole. And as evidenced by recent events even seemingly similar hotels have been impacted very differently depending upon a particular hotels management, location, accessibility and business mix.

Some hotels, in particular ones that have a diversified business mix and that have been able to tap into and maximize opportunities that have emerged from changing demand patters (i.e. changing fly vs drive, domestic vs international, and/or price value demand patterns etc.) have been able to rebuild business already.

The ability for other hotels, i.e. destination hotels in markets highly dependent upon air lift capacity, hotels in markets that are experiencing major declines in city wide base business, hotels that are dependent upon capturing demand and have limited ability to "induce" or generate demand etc.to rebuild business will be much more challenging. More recently and increasingly going forward, we can anticipate that hotel buyers and lenders will place much greater emphasis on the evaluation and underwriting of the underlying business mix/demand generators for a particular hotel in their investment and lending decisions.

VALUE CREATION AND PRESERVATION

A relatively low level of hotel transactions have occurred to date and few properties are available on the market. As a result, it is difficult for many hotel owners, investors or even shareholders to continue to grow their investments through external sources with accretion as a mandate. Strategies for most growth-oriented hotel companies, whether public or private, will need to emphasize income growth from internal methods.

Assess Enhancement Opportunities

Those with ownership interests in hotels must be prepared to develop and encourage their operators to create sustainable income improvement solutions from all of the real estate associated with the hotel. One beneficial tool that should be utilized in maximizing the overall value of a hotel is an exhaustive Value Creation and Preservation Strategy (VCPS). This tool identifies repositioning strategies, non-traditional revenue sources, commercial and/or retail leasing opportunities, excess land use alternatives, potential benefits of capital renovation and brand repositioning, highest-and-best-use analysis and improvements in property tax burden with the overall objective of maximizing the income output of the property.

Branding and Management

The analysis would identify alternative sources for branding and/or management and the value benefits expected from each option. Implementation of the recommendations will work to improve the asset's income producing capability from hotel operations and ultimately its value. It is important to understand that some agreements tied to a hotel could be considered an encumbrance and have an adverse effect on income and value. It is always beneficial to complete a thorough due diligence on all scenarios. This component of the analysis would also benefit the passive investor or owner by having a firm knowledgeable in-management practices monitoring performance.

Physical Evaluation

Another factor that also plays a significant role in the long-term value prospects of a hotel is its physical condition. A deteriorating property will result in lost market share and revenue as guests seek alternative accommodation. Loss of brand affiliation is also a potential detrimental effect of a deteriorating asset. The VCPS would outline the benefits of a continuous property reinvestment plan or complete renovation. It will force hotel operators to be proactive and gauge the physical condition of the competition and fully substantiate recommendations for capital improvements. The feasibility component of a VCPS would identify the potential upside to a capital renovation providing rationale for project financing.

Managing a capital renovation requires significant planning in order to minimize business disruption, reduce the potential for lost income during the renovation and deliver on time and on budget. The VCPS identifies key areas requiring planning and again rationalizes the expenditure by outlining its positive effect on income. The proper development of the renovation plan will address specific areas of expertise including architecture, engineering, legal, and construction and project management. A poorly implemented renovation can result in significant cost overruns, income erosion and destroy the desired investment returns.

Impact of New Supply

The economic life of a hotel can be adversely affected by the addition of new supply. In several cases, there have been new hotels built in markets that do not support development based on the local market operating statistics. However, some hotel developers have realized that the physical condition of the overall hotel stock within a certain market is inferior. These developers believe that a new property will steal market share from each existing hotel and on its own become successful leaving the poorest performers to suffer and possibly close or be converted to an alternative use. It is believed that this trend will continue as hotel franchisors push for brand presence in more markets. By working to develop the VCPS, a hotel owner can anticipate the effects that new supply will have on the value of their asset and devise a proactive strategy that minimizes the effect or reduces the possibility of new supply.

Hotel owners need to keep in mind that the emergence of alternative forms of competition will affect the value of their hotel investments. There has been a significant rise of indirect competition in the form of furnished apartments or condominiums in major markets across Canada. This competitor has taken market share from hotels in the fairly profitable extended stay segment. The real estate in which these businesses operate is typically residential affording these entities a significant tax advantage over hotels. This is a growing industry in many markets and is establishing structure but is not easily tracked. Owners need to monitor this and other forms of non-traditional indirect competition.

Other Components

Many hotels include other components that can have a significant impact on value but are often overlooked. An office or retail piece may be associated with a hotel property. These forms of real estate demand an understanding of local real estate trends in order to positively effect lease negotiations, vacancy rates and potential rental income. If an operator does not possess this expertise, it is difficult to constantly monitor activity in these areas. In addition, a highest-and-best use analysis may indicate that excess land or the overall site location would result in higher market value compared to its current use. The benefits of local market knowledge and real estate expertise can increase rental income and identify site potential to produce property value improvements.

Leasing out Components of the Operation

The opportunity to lease certain operating components within a hotel to a third party is an option that can improve a hotel's income. Some hotels have opted to lease out food and beverage operations, spas, golf courses and parking facilities to operators specializing in these disciplines. The benefit here is that the hotel now generates a more stable cash flow through lease income and the new operator will bring expertise that can improve service and product consistency. Property value can be enhanced with this arrangement since lease income is often more stable than income from operations.

Realty Tax Reduction

A successful property tax appeal can have a positive effect on a hotel's income. Often assessments on hospitality properties include a component of enterprise value. It is key in any assessment appeal to extract the business component from the real estate value. The value of furniture, fixtures and equipment and management skill must be extracted to reveal only the real estate value. Assessment experts will perform research and analysis to achieve the lowest possible assessed value.

This is a specialized area that is best handled by a realty company that offers professional property tax advice. A hotel operating business and its real estate components are closely interwoven. We have witnessed the negative impact that negligence or the mishandling of a hotel asset has on income and value. Regardless of whether you are preparing to refinance your asset, monetize equity, sell assets or boost cash flow it is beneficial to allow a real estate expert who understands the hotel industry develop a VCPS. This tool will address issues affecting a property with the goal of extracting maximum value while the hotel operator focuses on running a successful hotel.

COMPANY VALUATION

The purpose of company valuation is to measure the the "right value" of a business. The valuation of a business provides:

1. Review the performance of a business

2. Communicate to others (such as shareholders, investors, employees and the market) the value of firm's strategies and its results.

There are different methods of measuring the value of a Hotel business.

Equity based Method

The most basic method for a company is based solely on the values recorded in the firm's financial statements (balance sheets; profit and loss statement and cash flow management statements).

This method is based on the assumption the value of the firm is nothing but the sum of its assets, leaving aside the capacity of the company to generate values.

These methods provide for a quick evaluation of a company but presents with two major disadvantages -

— *Obsoleteness* - the information recorded in the financial statements reflects the state of the company at a given past time, thus, operations made by the company form that moment on, are not considered as providing of reducing value of the company. They do not consider company as an ongoing business.

— *Inaccurateness* - these methods are not able to take into consideration, the non-monetary value of managerial know how and company's innovation, as well as the firm's capacity to create value in the future, the required funds to maintain the company running, the market value of the assets and liabilities (as they are recorded at historic value), and the value of money in time. They can also be greatly influenced by the firms accounting policy, such as the use of last in first out (LIFO) or first in first out (FIFO) method for inventory valuation, the amortization of Goodwill, the realization of expenses, and the capitalization of cost.

Accounting-based Valuation

This kind of valuation takes into account the accounting information obtained from the company's balance sheets without performing any kind of adjustments. The value of the company is given by the difference between the total assets and total liabilities.

Corporate value = Total Assets - Total Liabilities

Adjusted Net Assets Valuation

This method tries to fix the historical evaluation method by making the following adjusts to the value of the assets by moving them toward the realization value by.

a.   Reduction of non-value assets [AssetsSNV] such as accrued charges and the cost of installation.

b.   The inclusion of those intangible assets [Int. assets] that provide for a value in the market, such as right to exercise a leasin

c.   The revaluation of fixed assets [AssetsSRV] as was going to be sold.

The value of the firm is than taken by

Corporate value = Adjusted net assets = [AssetsSRV + Int. assets] - [AssetsSNV + Liabilities]

Liquidation-based Method

This valuation approach supposes the termination of business under two different points of view.

—   A progressive sale of assets- Where the company is considered to be able to progressively sell its assets, and terminate operation in the far future. Assets are then valued at liquidation value [AssetLV]. Using this method, assets are priced at Lower value than their liquidation value, and some liquidation cost is not considered (such as penalty cost of personal dismissal, while the liabilities are kept at the book value.

— A forced liquidation of the company- This method provides for the liquidation of assets at the book value, but the liabilities are adjusted to include liquidation related obligations (such as personnel dismissal cost)

Corporate Value = [AssetLV] - (Liabilities)

Intrinsic Value or Usage Value

The most basic one form the buyer's perspective, considers the amount of fund required for rebuild the "company/ business" to its current state based on the replacement value of the assets.

Substantial Value

It represents the economic value for the buyer. The value of the company is computed by applying in the following rules.

— All assets are adjusted to their replacement value.

— All leased assets are included.

— All assets not required for operations are included.

Required Capital for Exploitation

This method considers the value of the company to be the value of the assets and funds required for operations. Do a proper SWOT (Strength, Weakness, Opportunity and Threats) of your business and its market and choose the right valuation method. Each method will give different result but a combined analysis of all will for sure give a good valuation result.

9

Hotel Marketing Management

One of the single greatest challenges facing independent hotels today is pricing. Pricing the inventory effectively can lead to profitability and helps lay the foundation for long term success. But, pricing the inventory ineffectively can lead to disaster.

The dilemma goes on and on because we have been using a market segment and pricing model that has not grown with the times. During the last decade, two simultaneous factors impacted the market place and customer buying practices: (1) the dramatic drop in demand (2) and the widespread use of the Internet for booking rooms. Capitalizing on this situation, third party Internet companies seized the opportunity to grow their businesses. Hotels were eager to work with them, and customers were eager to use them as confidence and security in buying goods and services on-line increased.

Historically, pricing was pretty straightforward. Pricing was set at one rate, Rack Rate. Those rates were posted on cards and placed in racks at the front desk. As technology became more sophisticated and hoteliers became more marketing savvy, market segments began to evolve. Each segment had its own buy decision and its own travel trends. An in-depth understanding and skillful integration of those segments placed the hotel in a greater position to maximize rates and occupancies. This was all made more manageable by the improved high tech nature of the newer hotel operating systems.

As the new technology was developing, corporate travel departments, as well as the independent consumer, turned to travel agents to get the best discounts. As the GDS technology influenced booking and buying practices, additional segments were created, resulting in the following market segment model:

— *Rack rates:* Without any affiliations to warrant discounts, the Rack Rated customer paid the published rate, which was the highest rate.

— *Consortia rates:* This was the same customer who booked through a travel agent using the GDS and received a 5%-10% discount off Rack Rates.

— *Corporate rates:* Having met the hotel's qualifying criteria, such as volume, businesses were guaranteed discounted rates.

— *Group rates:* With a block of rooms, rates varied based on time of year and the nature of the group.

— *Weekend rates:* Individual leisure travelers, usually within a drive distance to the hotel.

— *Promotional rates:* These rates were originally used sparingly and used as a means to stimulate business by using discounted rates to anyone, regardless of affiliation.

By understanding each segment and its role in the individual hotel, hoteliers created pricing and yield management systems and procedures which resulted in maximum performance.

— *Rack rates* were set to establish positioning; used as a basis for discounting; and used as a yield management tool for average rate maximization during high demand.

— *Consortia rates* were typically discounted 5%-10% off Rack Rates in order to capture a savvy traveler educated to ask for discounts through his/her travel agent, and to strengthen the travel agent's value to the customer.

— *Corporate rates* were negotiated to get year-round volume business for corporate accounts.

— *Group rates* were usually filler business and negotiated based on demand periods.

— *Promotional rates* were typically the lowest rates offered and are now being used on a daily basis.

But, as demand dramatically declined, independent hotels were most significantly impacted. In most cases, they did not have the financial resources and cooperative marketing opportunities of the chains. At the same time, the third party Internet booking companies were well positioned. Customer buying habits had changed significantly. As customers began to feel more secure in buying products and services online, use of the Internet become a tremendous resource for the consumer. As the third party Internet companies grew in popularity, independent hotels found a new source of business, with little expense involved.

What has now emerged is the realization that the Rack Rate segment no longer exists. The Internet has created- brand new distribution channels, directly reaching the end user and/or allowing the third party booking parties to profit as travel agents did until recently. The Internet booking companies, in order to ensure profitability, have adopted more of the airline pricing strategy, i.e. setting rates on a daily basis. These rates can vary significantly from day to day. The hotel industry will be hard pressed to revert to the old pricing model, now that the public has been conditioned to shop for prices.

Therefore, in order to respond to the changed market place relative to the Internet and to effectively compete against chain hotels as well as other independent hotels, flexible pricing is key. But in order for hotels to create and maintain pricing credibility, it is still important for hotels to move away from competing on price alone. This strategy has been universally unsuccessful and will always backfire.

Some suggested steps to realign rates and segments to the changed market place; gain control of business; and increase profitability are:

— Create an *online* booking presence.

— Ensure that the hotel's online booking engine is part of the hotel's web site, and controlled by the hotel, not by a third party or GDS-based system.

— Ensure that the online booking engine is the best and accomplishes the hotel's goals.

— Ensure that the online booking engine is easy to use from a customer's perspective.

— Expertly create and maintain an online distribution and maximization strategy to ensure the hotel's visibility.

— Promote and ensure that the lowest published rates are on the hotel's own web site, to promote customer loyalty, as done with the airlines.

— Establish a new market segmentation model, for greater control of the business. Eliminate RACK RATE and replace with SELL RATE, defined as Rack, Promotional, Consortia, and any other customer not affiliated with any discount.

— A simplified sample version is:
  — Sell rate
  — Corporate rate
  — Group rate
  — Weekend rate
— Establish the Sell Rate based on anticipated demand patterns, after the core business and group blocks are factored in. The rate fluctuates on a daily basis.
— Set rates in all market segments within the range of your competitive set to establish positioning.

By understanding how the Internet and customer buying habits have forever changed and how they impact the way hotels do business, will place owners and managers in a position of strength in managing the day to day business; achieving profitability; and demystifying many of the rate and segmentation questions.

HOTEL ACQUISITION

Given the complex nature of the interrelated business and real estate components of a hotel, the analysis and process of acquisition can be as complicated or as simple as the potential buyer wants to make it, recognizing that there are practical limitations to the human and financial resources that can be applied to a field of potential purchases. Conversely, there is a real benefit to added information and it is usually the most informed purchasers who get the best deals. The informed purchaser process through a series of steps designed to optimize the cost/benefit ratio of information. This phased acquisition process, each step of which is dealt with in the succeeding text, includes the following:

— Determining acquisition criteria

— Soliciting product
— Screening initial offerings and deciding upon targets
— Establishing a price and business plan
— Negotiating the deal to a contract or letter of intent
— Due diligence
— Closing the transaction

Criteria Determination

From the purely business standpoint, ownership rationale can vary from active to passive involvement. Some owners position strategically for the short term, while others take a longer view. In other instances, owners prefer to base their investment on yield or return requirements, which can vary, based on alternative investments available, strategic consideration, and other factors. Decision criteria are unique to each buyer. Among the criteria for deciding upon a hotel or group of properties to purchase are:

— Location
— Property type
— Size of property
— Cost
— Current and potential cash flow yield
— Potential appreciation in asset value
— Risk and stability of earnings
— Upside potential from repositioning, including renovation and/or management changes
— Ability for new competition to enter market
— Ability to replace management and/or franchise affiliation

There is no right or wrong answer for each asset. But no matter what the underlying motivation to purchase a hotel may be, a clearly defined strategy and decision process must be in place before entering into the acquisition process. This assures and informed judgment as to buyer motivations and market dynamics.

Identification of Acquisition Targets

After the acquisition criteria have been decided upon, the buyer will typically get work into the market that he is interested in acquiring hotels that meet specified criteria. Brokers, asset managers, hotel companies and industry consultants are among those contacted. Often, press releases and advertisements in trade publication and the general business press are used to "get the word out".

Once the request for properties has gone out, the buyer will then screen preliminary offerings submitted to him while continuing to network with industry professionals for hints of properties about to go on the market before they are "shopped around". The screening process is crucial, as it allows the elimination of numerous properties early on and sets the stage for substantial effort be expended on other properties. Too often the buyer overlooks the screening step and misses good opportunities and expends unnecessary effort in the long run.

Lacking his own screening team, the buyer can call upon a team of outside due diligence/acquisition consultants. At his early stage in the process the buyer can "pick their brains" as to their general knowledge of potentially available properties. Using experience consultants with local market knowledge can materially help both in the screening and in the negotiation and acquisition phases.

Acquisition Team

Given the hotel's dual nature as both a business and real estate, an investor should be sure to have the advice of those familiar with the hotel industry. Typically, and investor will assemble a team of about six professionals who will assist in the overall evaluation of a hotel property. Such a team would include the following:

— *Broker.* The broker may represent either the buyer or seller of a lodging property. The broker typically helps market a property and bring the seller and buyer together. Often the broker helps negotiate and facilitate a sale. A broker's fee is typically a percentage of the total sales price.

— *Appraiser.* Since the work experience of potential appraisers can vary widely, it is advisable to select an appraiser who has appraised either similar properties or properties in the market in question.

— *Accountant.* An Accountant's review of the property's books and record will determine whether funds have been properly applied and whether financial controls and reporting systems are adequate.

— *Market & Financial Consultant.* A market and financial consultant is called upon to ascertain how a property might perform and what it would take to achieve desired profit or investment goals. Such consultants evaluate prevailing market conditions, prepare projections for both the market and the subject property. The market and financial consultant can also review revenues and expenses and assist in assembling the business plan.

— *Attorney/Legal Consultant.* Attorneys specializing in hotel work can help formulate the acquisition strategy or game plan, assist in identifying and coordinating acquisition team members, advise on terms and structure of transactions, assist in legal due diligence issues from the significance of litigation and regulatory matters, contracts, title issues, and document and close what is often not merely a "vanilla" real estate deal, but the purchase and sale of a complex real estate/business transaction. At a minimum, these are likely to include hospitality operation, management and franchise, labor, real estate, tax, corporate, and trademark. In other situations litigation bankruptcy, timeshare and other specialties may be critical.

— *Architects/Designers.* If the acquisition is to involve renovation or upgrading of the property, the architect will be responsible for reviewing the specifications set forth by the owner, as well as reviewing the applicable codes or regulations of the state or local municipalities. In addition, an architect can coordinate the activities of other members of the team who will be responsible for the physical property, such as the engineer and interior designer. He can review existing and potential compliance with all building codes as they apply to the existing property and as they will apply to any planned renovations.

— *Engineer.* A qualified engineer or team of engineers should review all the physical components of the property, including mechanical, electrical, plumbing, and structural elements.

Evaluation of Acquisitions

Many properties will be weeded out during the initial screening process, based primarily on review of submitted offering packages, the buyer's or consultant's knowledge, and the acquisition criteria itself. For those properties that pass this initial screening, the next step is usually a site visit an property inspection at which point another "go/no-go" decision will be make. Properties that reach the inspection stage will require a preliminary property and market analysis. The next decision, based on the analysis, will be to develop a bid price and business plan or to eliminate the property from consideration.

Perhaps the most significant element in the buyer's development of a purchase price is the analysis of the potential earnings to be derived from the hotel. In many purchases, it's the only element. T develop the proposed acquisition price, the buyer must make assumptions as to future market conditions and the hotel's performance within that market. These assumptions will be reflected in a discounted cash flow or stabilized operating projection. Thus, a preliminary business plan which reflects assumptions as to physical facilities and condition, management, affiliation and other factors must be developed in order to assess the potential acquisition realistically.

Understanding the Market

That markets will change is a given. Factors causing such a change include growth or decline in the supply of hotel rooms, shifts in market segmentation, and the renovation or repositioning of competitive hotels. The prudent hotel buyer understand the concept of property and market dynamics and does not purchase without a plan in place for receiving an expected return of his investment over time. This plan will reflect research and analysis on historical market performance, expectations for the growth in the supply of competitive hotel rooms, and the growth in demand for hotel by market segment (commercial, leisure, group etc.) by guest ability and willingness to pay at the projected rate level, and guest demands as to facilities, design concepts, amenities and services.

Facilities

— Design concept
— Configuration
— Mix of guest rooms and suites
— Restaurants and lounges
— Banquet and meeting space
— Recreational facilities
— Parking
— Other Facilities
— Materials used relative to maintenance and durability
— Compliance with current and proposed building and other codes

Identification

— Name
— Franchise or brand affiliation, evaluated in light of its contribution in terms of number of room nights and price/value perception

Management

The management company or organization will be the one best suited to the needs of the property vis a vis quality, operating culture, cost control and marketing strengths

Capital Structure and Financing Costs

After reviewing historical and projected market performance, along with the historical performance of the subject property relative to that market, the potential buyer will evaluate and plan for each of the foregoing issues. The result will be a set of assumptions as to future market performance, a plan of action for the property, and a set of cash flow projections resulting from that plan. The Cash flow projections, including assumptions as to capital expenditures and reserves, financing costs, an exit strategy and disposition price, will then be discounted back to a present values at a discount rate that meets the buyer's return requirement. In this way, the buyer establishes the price he is willing to pay for the subject property.

Taken as a whole, the analysis outlined above, will help the buyer determine how next to proceed: whether an appropriately priced buy represents a turnaround opportunity with great upside potential, or whether the hotel as already reached its maximum earnings level, thus posing a significant downside risk to the investment.

In determining an offering price for the subject property, the prudent buyer will consider the foregoing discounted cash flow analysis, the historical earnings of the property, and the sales prices per room being achieved for comparable hotel sales in the marketplace. The relationship of the offering price to the discounted cash flow analysis is often dependent upon the strength of the market, the buyer's and seller's relative positions, and other market factor. The stronger the seller's market, the higher the offer price, and vice versa.

Once the potential buyer makes the initial offer, negotiations begin. The resulting process will either wind up with the buyer and seller coming to a meeting of the minds on the purchase price and continuing into more refined discussions or the negotiations will be broken off.

Once an agreement to purchase has been reached, the buyer will often summarize for internal approval or other purposes the analysis which led to the decision. The resulting investment memorandum may include the following:

— Property Description
— Market summary, past and projected
— Projected profit and loss and cash flow statements for the property, with a business plan and key assumptions as to:
— Management style
— Affiliation
— Marketing
— Operating costs
— Capital expenditures, with schedule and major categories
— Financing
— Other elements of any proposed repositioning

Purchase and Sale Agreement Process

After a tentative agreement to buy and sell has been reached, the process of negotiating the major terms of the purchase and sale agreement can begin. Successfully negotiating and preparing a contract for the purchase or sale of real estate requires a thorough understanding of the objectives of the buyer or seller, the legal and tax situation, the character of the property and the interest of third parties, including lenders, brokers, union etc., who may require contractual provisions for their protection even though they are not parties to the contract.

The basic terms of sale, along with a property inspection, enable the purchaser to determine if the price and terms are reasonable and if the property is worth purchasing and make an initial offer.

Because the purchase and sale of real estate involves the investment of a substantial sum of money and the transfer of valuable assets, the parties and their professional advisors should negotiate the terms of the transaction with great care and precision.

Detailed discussion should include the following crucial business elements of the deal:

— The purchase price and any adjustments
— Third-party financing, whether existing at the time of the transaction or to be arranged by the buyer
— Purchase money financing by the seller
— Condition of the premises
— Limitations on title and possession
— No shop provision
— Default by either party
— Indemnifications
— Items included and excluded from the purchase price

The business nature of hotels dictates that a great many assets other than pure real estate would be included to make it a going concern. Likewise, the negotiation of the transaction and the items included and excluded has a substantial impact on the flow and cost of transition from old owner to new owner.

As a general rule, hotel assets include the following:

Current Assets

— Cash
— Accounts Receivable
— Prepaid Expenses
— Securities

— Inventories of food and beverage
— Inventories of supplies
— Printing and stationery
— Other current assets

Property and Equipment

— Land
— Building and improvements
— Furniture, fixtures and equipment
— Linen, china, glassware, silverware and uniforms

Other Assets

— Organizational costs
— Pre-Opening expenses
— Other deferred charges
— Deposits
— Licenses and permits

Non-financial assets are also a consideration in a hotel acquisition. Accounting books and records, operating statistics, employee records, sales and marketing files, licenses and permits and numerous other items are required to keep a hotel going. The hotel buyer should be certain to have his attorney and operational advisors assist in making sure that the purchase terms will ensure a smooth operation transition form seller to buyer.

Price

Final sales price is often affected by negotiations involving other terms in the purchase and sale contract,. For example, the purchaser will at times pay a higher price if the seller is willing to take back purchase money financing. Other factors that can influence final sales price are the amount of the earnest money deposit, the amount of time over which cash payments can be spread, and whether or not an existing mortgage can be assumed. Other considerations that may affect final sales price include the track record and financial strength of the purchaser and the speed with which the transaction can be completed and what is being purchased.

Existing Management or Franchise Affiliation

When a hotel is subject to a hotel management contract, the contract should be examined by counsel to determine ability to assign, terminate or otherwise deal with it. When the purchaser desires a new operator, the parties must resolve the ability to terminate and related issues of canceling the management contract. In some instances, the contract can be terminated by paying a cancellation fee. Generally, when a hotel is sold without the requirement that the existing management be retained, the sale price will be higher than it would be if the operator were to remain.

Contingencies

In situations where the seller is the present management company operating the property, and the purchaser wants the management company to remain in place, the seller may offer cash flow guarantees or take-back purchase money financing, which essentially pays out the purchase price over time. Such arrangements generally create a higher selling price and make it easier for the purchase to put together the overall financing.

When a buyer enters into a purchase and sale contract, a sizable money deposit is usually made to demonstrate the purchaser's commitment to closing the transaction. If the deal is not completed, the buyer may forfeit all or a portion of the deposit. To reduce the risk of losing the deposit, the purchaser usually negotiates a set of key terms involving various contingencies that allow the purchaser to back out of the transaction and still have all or a portion of the deposit returned.

Some of the more frequently used contingencies include any inability of the purchaser to:

— Obtain specified financing
— Transfer or obtain a specified franchise affiliation
— Obtain specified licenses or permits (particularly a liquor license)
— Approve results of complete due diligence within a specified period of time
— Obtain clear legal title to the hotel's real property

In a seller's market or where the seller has a choice among buyers, the seller usually agrees to encumber a transaction with one or more of these contingencies only as a result of negotiations that entitle the seller to receive such benefits as a higher price or more favorable terms.

Contract Issues

One school of thought holds that a letter of intent is the best way to start the process of buying or selling a property. Most parties do not intend a letter of intent to be a binding contract; nevertheless, the letter on intent can be a binding contract if that intention is indicated and sufficient terms are specified. It lays out the basic terms of the agreement; it also serves as an obligation on the part of both the buyer and seller to make an effort in good faith to complete the transaction. After the letter of intent has been accepted by both parties, the buyer must perform tasks of due diligence and must obtain financing. Negotiations regarding the final form of the purchase and sale contract should be ongoing throughout the entire process. When the content, structure and schedule of the transition are agreed upon the closing takes place.

Unless the letter of intent provides otherwise (and the provision is stated to be binding) the seller can negotiate with other interested investors. The investor has to make a good faith effort to conclude the transaction. Ethically, this restricts the seller to a limited extent. Nevertheless, letters of intent may serve a legitimate purpose in the following situations:

— If one of the parties is an institution or investment group, a policy may require a letter of intent before negotiations can proceed (in order to minimize legal and other expenses or to minimize the risk of undue publicity if the transaction fails to close).

— If the transaction is to be financed by the public issuance of securities, the underwriting concern may require a letter of intent as a "comfort document" to justify the time and expense in a due diligence investigation.

— In a complex negotiation that may take many months to complete, a letter of intent may prevent misunderstandings by identifying the purposes of the parties at the inception of the negotiation.

The following list contains items that might be included in a letter of intent.

— *Property Description* A description of the property being sold or leased. This is not a legal description, but is detailed so that both parties understand the nature of the transaction.

— *Selling Price* A description of the price and terms of the transaction and the financing structure.

— *Due Diligence* The purchaser is allowed to perform a certain amount of review, documentation, and analysis of the property.

— *Contingencies* Specific circumstances that allow one or both of the parties to void the deal.

— *Seller's Representations* Representations that are made regarding the owner's legal ability to complete the transaction.

Depending upon the language used and legal doctrines that may apply, this document can be (1) binding, (2) non-binding, or (3) partly binding and partly non-binding. The typical letter of intent attempts to detail only the most important deal points to be sure the parties have fundamental agreement of the "big issues" before they proceed with due diligence and definitive contract negotiation. When a letter of intent is intended to be non-binding in its entirety, it is usually just a preliminary step used to confirm a meeting of the minds on key terms before expending more time and money on due diligence and documentation.

A binding letter of intent can be dangerous, because any party may be able to compel the other party to perform without agreement on the details that are usually worked out in the final definitive agreement. However, a letter of intent is often intended to be binding only in certain regards and otherwise non-binding. This is the case where the parties want to postpone negotiations of the details to a later time, but want certain provisions to be binding, such as a forfeitable deposit by buyer, confidentiality provisions, a "no shop" provision.

The language of the letter of intent is very important in determining what provisions, if any, are binding and what provisions are non-binding. Parties should be advised by counsel whether they want a letter of intent to be binding in whole or in part, or to be non-binding in whole or in part. For a letter of intent to form a binding contract, it should expressly state that intention and it must also specify sufficiently the material terms of agreement such as parties, subject matter, price, and terms. If the parties want a letter of intent to be non-binding, that intention should also be clear. But in many states, the law will imply conditions on the parties that they may not have intended or understood. For example, a buyer or seller may believe a letter of intent is non-binding, but may not be free to walk away from the deal without negotiating in good faith with the other party to consummate the transaction. If the parties want to be able to terminate at any time without damages, then a clause should be added to that specific effect. Similarly, since a buyer may expend substantial money in due diligence, he should understand what rights, if any, he has to force the seller to proceed with the sale.

Another school of though hold that a letter of intent just wastes time that could be better spent in negotiation a binding definitive agreement with appropriate "outs" or conditions such as satisfactory due diligence, obtaining financing, obtaining necessary regulatory approvals, compliance with the pre-acquisition requirement of the Hart-Scott-Rodino Act and other such matters. Under this approach, the parties execute a binding agreement of purchase and sale and simply provide that the agreement may be terminated (with or without payment of certain sums) in specified events prior to the expiration of the due diligence period.

Once under binding contract, a buyer may have greater comfort in spending the money required to complete due diligence, obtain financing, and take the other steps necessary to buy the property. The down-side of this approach is the time and money required to negotiate the agreement without the certainty that the diligence results will be satisfactory or that other condition will be satisfied.

The parties may seek to insure that the letter of intent is not legally binding by expressly providing that no legal obligation will be incurred by either party unless evidenced by a formal written contract. Despite this, it is possible that one party may end up liable in damages to the other on the basis that the obligation to negotiate in good faith was breached. If the parties wish to avoid any such interpretation the letter of intent should include a specific provision that neither party has a duty to continue negotiating and that either prorate may withdraw from negotiations for any reason.

Purchase and Sale Contract

The final purchase and sale contract negotiations should establish the complete terms and condition of the transaction. The issues covered in the purchase and sale contract include all those in the letter of intent and many other details that typically not included in a letter of intent, particularly representations and warranties, indemnifications, and closing conditions and terms. With any contract, the actual document should be reviewed and approved by an attorney and an accountant familiar with hotel and real estate transactions to ensure that none of the terms conflict with federal, state or local laws.

The basic clauses usually found in a purchase and sale contract are as follows:

— *Real and Personal Property Being Sold.* A description of the real and personal property being transferred.

— *Business Assets Being Sold.* A listing of the various licenses, contracts, franchises, and other miscellaneous and intangible personal property that are being transferred with the real property.

— *Closing.* The date, time and place of closing.

— *Purchase Price.* The purchase price and its composition

— *Earnest Money or Deposit.* The amount of the deposit and circumstances under which it would be defaulted or returned.

— *Due Diligence.* The review of the property and other aspects of the transaction made by the purchaser and the conditions and limits imposed upon the transaction. The contract should detail the period of time during which this should occur and the rights and obligations of each party.

— *Terms of Purchase Financing.* The terms of the mortgage involved in transactions in which the seller takes back purchase money.

— *Title Commitment and Survey/Search.* The specifications for the type and quality of title the purchaser is willing to accept.

— *Seller's Deliveries.* The data and information that must be given to the purchaser by the seller.

— *Seller's Representation, Warranties and Covenants.* The various facts and statements made by the seller relative to the transaction which are used to induce the purchaser to buy the property.

— *Representations and Warranties of Purchaser* The various facts and statements made by the purchaser relative to the transaction which are used to induce the seller to sell the property.

— *Prorations and Adjustments.* The specific prorations of the current revenues and expenses between the purchaser and seller.

— *Closing documents and procedures.* The various documents needed to close the transaction as agreed to by both parties. The closing procedure must also be approved by both parties.

— *Closing Expense.* The agreement reached on the allocation of closing expenses between the purchaser and seller.

— *Eminent Domain and Risk of Loss.* The details of what occurs if the property is taken by eminent domain or a casualty loss while the hotel is under contract.

— *General Clauses.* General housekeeping contract clauses.

Employee Issues

Since much of a hotel's success is based on the expertise and cordiality of its employees, compassionate treatment of employees during the often stressful sale period can go along way toward protecting the business being purchased. Unfortunately, however, the liability for past employment practices for the seller and/or future employment practices of the buyer usually motivate both parties to make the separation as dramatic as possible.

It is usually preferable for the buyer to have previous ownership officially terminate all employees on the day of takeover and for the new entity to re-hire them on a probationary basis. At the same time, an analysis can be made of medical and health benefits, pension and retirement plans, vacation and sick day entitlements, etc. If appropriate, the buyer may choose to allow all employees to carry their benefits forward as if no sale had taken place, with an accounting between buyer and seller for the accrued liabilities for vacation, sick days and retirement assumed by the buyer. Legal counsel can help a buyer avoid unintended "successor liability" for employment practices of the seller or its predecessors.

Legal guidance is particularly important where a hotel is the subject of union contracts, union organization activity or some unique plant closing laws.

Due Diligence

A thorough analysis of the financial condition of the hotel is usually termed a Due Diligence Review, or simply, "due diligence." Any letter of intent or purchase and sale agreement should provide that purchaser's obligation are subject to satisfactory results from the due diligence investigation. A Due Diligence Review would typically deal with the following items.

— External annual audited profit and loss statements, with full supporting schedules, for the last five years.

— Current year to date profit and loss statement with comparison to previous year.

— Monthly profit and loss statements, with full supporting schedules for the past three years.

— Audited balance sheet for the last five years.

— Occupancy and average rate the last three years.

— Capital expenditures for the last five years, with any current projections for expenditures.

— All architectural and engineering plans and specifications.

— All inspection reports, including health, fire, building and elevator.

— Copies of all studies, including all recent appraisals, market studies, environmental/engineering reports and marketing plans.

— List of all tenants, rent rolls, deposits and term of lease.

— Inventory of FF&E, supplies, consumables and inventories.

— Real and personal property tax bills for the last three years.

— Schedule of all insurance coverage, including cost and expiration.

— The legal property description.

— Copies of all service contracts, leases, franchises, licenses, permits, management agreements, union agreements and any instruments that the purchaser is expected to assume.

— Copies of all trademarks, trade names and copyrights.

— Copies of all notes and mortgages currently encumbering the property.

— Details of any administrative action or litigation threatened or pending against the hotel.

— Estoppel letters from any mortgage.

— A list of employees, including name, position salary and benefits.

— A list of future reservations and bookings, including name of party, deposit received, rate guaranteed, dates and status.

— List of all purveyors and sources of supplies and services.

Tasks performed during the due diligence process include:

— *Financial Audit* - an independent audit performed by accountant or firm with experience in the hospitality industry.

— *Engineering Inspection* - a detailed study of all physical components of the property, including mechanical, electrical, plumbing, structural elements, telephone systems, computer systems and items of decor.

— *Environmental Inspection* - a detailed inspection made by a qualified environmental engineer to disclose any potential environmental hazards that may exist on or within the property site.

— *Legal Verification* - an investigation by a skilled local attorney into all the property's contracts, licenses, permits, franchises and other documents to determine any potential adverse provisions and whether they can be transferred from the seller to the buyer.

— *Title Search* - a review of the various factors that could affect the title to a property. The title search should be performed by either an attorney or title company.

— *Property Tax Verification* - a search into the current status of the tax assessment imposed on the property. When a hotel property is sold, the local taxing jurisdiction is likely to investigate the terms of the sale and possible adjust the property's assessed value upward to reflect the sale price. A new assessed value could adversely affect the property's future cash flow. A property tax verification performed by a knowledgeable property tax consultant will provide an accurate estimate of future tax liabilities. The property tax consultant can also assist in minimizing an upward adjustment made by the assessor.

The closing of a hotel transaction involves the actual transfer of title of the hotel from the seller to the buyer. Generally, when the buyer assumes management, the closing coincides with the takeover by the new operator. The parties that are normally present at a closing include:

— Seller and seller's attorney

— Buyer and buyer's attorney

— Lender and lender's attorney

— Title company

— Real estate broker

The activities that take place at a closing include accounting to allocate and prorate the property's revenues and expenses and a physical inventory of all the assets included in the purchase price. Any items to be transferred that are not included in the purchase price must be inventoried and valued in accordance with the terms of the purchase and sale contract. After the necessary allocations and prorations are calculated, the mortgages and notes are signed and the requisite moneys are transferred among the parties. Once this process is concluded, the buyer holds title to the hotel.

DIRECT SALES

Hotels across every segment of the industry today are faced with the challenge of delivering profits in an ever-changing environment of declining revenues and profitability. Independently owned and operated hotels have the added challenge of limited marketing resources. As a result, owners and managers of independent properties, now, more than ever, have to ensure that each marketing expense is justified and that it produces the best return on investment.

Direct Sales typically represents 40-50% of the entire marketing expense budget. As a result, with up to 50% of the marketing budget devoted to this one line item, it is critical to ensure that each sales person is effective and productive in achieving short term results and in laying the foundation for success in the long term.

Out of all the elements of the marketing plan, Direct Sales is the most controllable and quantifiable element. In order to achieve maximum production, it is critical to:

— Hire, train, and expertly direct the best sales people.

— Implement systems to ensure optimal productivity and individual accountability.

— Develop and maintain action plans and goals which are targeted, specific, and proactive.

Success in today's market is accomplished by a different game plan than when demand was at its peak. Therefore, in order to ensure effectiveness, it is useful to start with several key concepts:

Sales is a skill, not a personality trait. How many times have we hired personable and attractive people only to find out that they are not effective in booking business? We discover that tentative bookings rarely become definites and that any client complaint can send the sales person over the moon!

Skills are required in any other profession and in any other department in the hotel in order to perform the job. Many times, we look to hire a sales person with a "rolodex" without considering his/her ability to sell, i.e., identifying business for the property and moving that business from another hotel. Client contacts can quickly come and go, resulting in an obsolete rolodex, but effective sales skills will result in constant business and on-going client relationships.

Expert sales skills can produce business despite product deficiencies, rate structure, or market conditions. Since most owners and operators do not have perfect properties, it is even more critical to ensure that each sales person is highly skilled to generate business and to deal with client objections and problems effectively. A dedication to expert sales skills is the best insurance for market share and profitability.

Direct sales is responsible for maximising rate and occupancy. Who would argue with that statement? But without properly structuring and organizing the sales department, and without establishing all elements of the rooms business, rate and occupancy will more often than not be compromised. Unlike many other industries, our product is perishable and is constant. The room we do not sell today is forever gone and conversely, in high demand, we cannot sell more rooms than we have. We have to make the most of what we have. Therefore, with proper planning and through expertise, we can let strong market conditions fill our rooms during certain, days, weeks, or months without incurring any costs or wasting valuable sales time and resources. By understanding market segmentation and supply/demand dynamics, the sales effort can be maximized by focusing on impacting business for gap periods, not during peak periods which require no effort or resources to fill.

The hotel, as part of its planning and over-all strategy, must determine what segments of the market will produce the best mix of business on a daily basis and translate that information into sales action plans and sales goals. Working with and understanding each market segment will determine those segments for which direct sales is responsible. A detailed plan or rooms budget will provide the basis for an effective sales plan.

One responsibility of direct sales is to create an account base by prospecting for new business and maintaining existing business. Production of this quantified business will fluctuate so it is important that new accounts are opened and non-producing ones are closed, ensuring that targeted goals are continuously reached.

Incentive programmes are a great way to motivate and get better results. But in order to ensure that all bookings represent the hotel's best financial interest, it is important to incorporate the cycle of demand periods. Otherwise, the incentive programme is ineffective if sales people can achieve their individual goals at the expense of the hotel's revenue potential.

Above-average leadership will produce above-average results. All world-class athletes recognize the importance of leadership and coaching in order to achieve top performances. Therefore, to ensure maximum results, effective sales and marketing leadership is required. At the hotel level, a leader is one who understands the big picture and can plan and organize as well as understand and implement the details to consistently accomplish the goals, despite market conditions. In small boutique hotels, there may not be a director of sales. In that case, leadership is still important and can be fulfilled by a general manager, a corporate sales person, or an outside sales specialist.

Sales plans are devised after a well thought-out marketing plan is established. Sales accountability is important to ensure results. As part of the planning, it is important for hotel leadership to establish and maintain systems and procedures to monitor productivity of each sales person on an on-going and timely basis.

Setting goals and keeping score is important. We all know that a golf game and a tennis match are much more interesting when we keep score; and we all perform better when our competitive juices are challenged. Even the Weight Watchers Programme has determined that weight loss is more effective with the weekly "weigh-in" to measure the results of the individual's efforts.

To maximize the sales person's performance, it is important to establish specific and meaningful goals, broken down on a monthly and weekly basis; and to establish a culture where the actual performance vs. goals is critical for job performance. Set goals which include activities to produce booked and consumed business as well as booking and consumed rooms goals. On-going and consistent monitoring and evaluation will foster performance and will quickly help identify non-performers.

With the above components in place and a true understanding and dedication to the elements of Direct Sales, every owner and manager is well positioned to achieve targeted financial results, efficiently and cost effectively.

Asset Value of a Hotel Brands

To solidify the advantage of an appreciating brand asset, it is fundamental to the success of branded hotels to master the dynamics of marketing management and operations management. A balanced approach is discussed and its model presented with the purpose of helping achieving brand integrity and consistency.

The integrity of any brand rides on doing well what the brand says and saying it right what the brand does every day at every point of guest contact. The most successful hotel brands understand that their value proposition must be relevant to their targeted customers and that they have to successfully differentiate themselves from their competitors. To achieve this, a hotel operator can choose to compete in any category or classification as long as there is brand clarity. What would that mean? It means guests easily identify a brand symbol or logo, are familiar with the brand's concept and knowledgeable enough to expect a certain set of benefits, which matter to them.

A frequent mistake is seen when hotels choose to compete only on rates. On the one hand the guests may flip their brand loyalty to price loyalty, on the other hand the price parity of an intangible product (room night) is a delicate issue. Hotel operators work so hard to earn the market recognition of their brand – all this credibility can be thrown out the window the moment a quality brand chooses to ask the customer the rate of lesser product.

Model of Brand Asset Equilibrium

Branding has implications on each facets of hotel management. However, the management of marketing and the management of operations are the most critical in this regard. Different levels of management have to work together as a team to achieve a balance between these two categories because the brand asset value is riding on this delicate balance.

Lodging brands develop a set of standards to ensure the consistency and integrity of the services they offer. All the standards regarding property curb-appeal, guest service procedures, the maintenance of fixtures, furniture, equipment and providing a specific line of supplies can be strictly followed. However, clean carpets or the finest towels alone cannot guarantee fair market share. If the marketing of the hotel is not managed adequately, the hotel may not have a clear understanding of its strengths, weaknesses, opportunities and threats compared to its set of competing properties; the market of the hotel may be not be well segmented, target markets not be properly identified and the hotel's offerings may not be effectively communicated and promoted. When a hotel's positioning and promoting are inadequate, as a result the brand asset value may start to slip.

Right message, wrong remedy: When one of the leading international upper-midscale brands launched an excellent service promise campaign in 2002, the brand promised a discount to guests for service failures. Why is this initiative not necessarily helping to grow brand asset value?

If marketing and operations were well aligned, it would have been obvious that

1. A significant portion of their clientele consists of business travelers. A cash discount to these travelers is not meaningful (relevant) to them.

2. It is not enough to identify mistakes. They should be eliminated through preventive actions.

The brand asset value may start to slip for the following reasons:

— The offered compensation is not meaningful to the brand's key customers;

— The apologies and corrective actions are expected anyway without campaign commitments;

— The marketing campaign invites the guests attention towards failures and mistakes in operation; and

— A successful alignment of the marketing message of the campaign with operations should include a follow-up both on the operational side (to ensure the mistake will not be repeated) and on the guest relations side.

The fact that the service guarantee programme reached its second year means that the brand could not successfully eliminate the recurring mishaps although they were identified at the outset. If a brand would choose to differentiate itself by the level of service, discounts may not be a useful part of a marketing campaign.

What are the consequences of being marketing-heavy and light in operations? In this case a "say-do gap" develops: marketing communications tells consumers what to expect from a brand but their experiences with the brand may not live up to those expectations. One never gets a second chance to make a good first impression: if a hotel's reservations department is understaffed and the caller is put on hold for long minutes, the future guest can quickly figure it out how important the call is to the hotel.

Right attention to the wrong guest: a guest who asked for a late check-out and got it granted by the Front Office, finds in the morning his invoice discreetly slipped in under the door. Nice touch; a courtesy for early departures, who are in a rush. Although well intended, the message is clear: the hotel either did not log the request or forgot to let the cashier (or night clerk) know about it. Either way: the guest is under the impression that this hotel's right hand has no clue what its left one is doing (a late check-out vs. an early departure). The operations of a hotel must do more than simply produce satisfied customers; they must reinforce the brand's value proposition at every point of contact. As a result of an imbalance, the brand asset value may start to slip.

Nobody is perfect and mistakes can be costly. A hotel guest of a luxury hotel who requested a room with a view, complained at check-out. The front desk learned that although the room was carefully assigned on a high floor with the best angle towards the sights, the tinted windows were less than perfect. Cracks and air pockets between the thin layers of the protective tinted film on the outside of the window pane caused some distortion as the guest explained. Apologies and rebates were offered and an upgrade on return. But most importantly: the hotel had to do something about those window panes to prevent future complaints.

If a hotel operator chooses to thrive for perfection, every mistake in operations will be costly and the brand asset value may start to slide in the eye of the demanding customer. If an economy hotel advertises vending machines on the premises and guests find it out of stock, more can be lost than the margin on a can of pop: the loyalty of a guest.

The Equilibrium

It is fair to say that the brand can be one of the most valuable assets a company can own. So far the presented model concentrated on the corporate side of the cohesion. Successful brands are perceived to gain a high level of awareness in the mind of the customer, therefore a brand asset equilibrium model should also include the customer-side relationships. These items are the strength and the stature of a brand. Marketing and operations play synergistic roles in driving brand asset value. No brand can be successful without building a base of loyal and satisfied customers who hold the brand in high regard (stature). A hotel brand can be strong in the eye of the customer if it does what it says consistently, it can be clearly differentiated from others and if its value proposition is relevant to its guests (strength). The relevancy of product attributes is always specific to a given hotel and its clientele. To the guests of a budget category motel a well signaled easy access to the property from a highway and free parking can be just as important as premium cable channel selection and ice machines on the guest floors. To the corporate traveler guest of an upper-midscale property a rolling 24-hours check-out time policy, high-speed wireless internet access with easy connectivity and round-the-clock room service would be more relevant than free local calls.

Co-ops, Consortiums and Clusters

When the hospitality industry is in a downturn such as in the early 1990s and after September 11, 2001, there is an accelerated interest in achieving efficiencies. For many years prior to the 1990s downturn and more so thereafter co-ops were one form of marketing efficiency used in advertising, promotions or sales. In addition to co-ops, consortiums emerged as yet another form of marketing efficiency. Consortiums were formed or joined by many hospitality organizations in areas such as reservations, travel intermediaries (i.e., agencies), airlines, (code sharing/capacity sharing), and also in areas outside of marketing. Another product of the pursuit of efficiencies was the concept of clusters.

Clusters in the marketing area include lodging facilities in the same market area; commingling their sales activities, sharing leads and sales calls. After 9/11 clusters began to emerge not only for purposes of sales and marketing efficiencies but in other functional areas as well. In this section, let us look at the benefits, drawbacks, and potential pitfalls involved with each concept. Since these three terms are sometimes used interchangeably, let's begin with a definition of each for clarification purposes.

First, a co-op in marketing in the hospitality business is usually defined as "an agreement between two or more businesses providing funding for marketing (advertising) or other mutually advantageous objectives." An example would be an objective to increase business to Hawaii. The cooperative agreement might be structured between an airline, resort, and rental car company to jointly fund and advertise a package (two or more components of a trip) to Hawaii. Each could advertise only their respective brand, however, there are considerable efficiencies to be gained by advertising together. And, the consumer buying the Hawaii destination often looks for a package. Each member of the co-op if they went it alone, planned to spend $100,000 in select newspaper ads. By combining their ad and funds, they now have $300,000 available for advertising in the newspapers. In essence, three times as many ads (or space) than if they went it alone. This is an oversimplification, but makes the point about efficiencies and how a co-op works.

Second, a consortium is defined as "a group (of companies or brands) formed to undertake an enterprise beyond the resources of any one member and/or for greater benefits and/or efficiencies than available by oneself." For example, two or more firms decide to form a consortium for purchasing to reap the benefits of economies of scale in buying products/services each of the firms use. These products/services could range from bars of soap to reservation services. A few variations of this concept include membership or partnership in an electronic e-procurement group to the actual formation of an independent company to perform services for all equity partners. An example of the latter, is Avendra. Avendra is an independent company formed early in 2001 by Marriott International, Hyatt Corporation, ClubCorp USA, InterContinental Hotels Group, and Fairmont Hotels and Resorts, all formidable entities in the hospitality industry. Avendra's purpose is to leverage the buying power for these companies and help each gain greater efficiencies. Not only are there economies of scale, there are other benefits as well. For example, staff reductions, customized product, and lower prices top the list.

The third concept to be defined is the cluster. In general, a cluster is "provision for a single point of control for management of similar brands, properties and/or functions within a given geographic area." For example, Hilton, with multiple products and brands has formed a Houston cluster. This cluster is directed by the general manager of the Houston Post Oak Doubletree (one of Hilton's brands). The cluster consists of four managed properties including three Doubletree hotels and one Hilton. The cluster also enjoys the participation of ten franchised partners. This cluster covers the areas of loss prevention, security, human resources, engineering, and sales and marketing. Additionally, the clusters finance, food and beverage, front office, purchasing, and revenue management departments. All have been active in providing cost savings and adding value.

Be it co-ops, consortiums, and/or clusters, Hilton is not alone in the hospitality industry in these practices. Marriott, Starwood, numerous airlines and others have all experimented or put into practice some or many elements of these efficiency concepts.

Just as the headlines read many in the hotel industry see each of these three concepts as win win scenarios. There certainly are identifiable efficiencies and results that can be measured. There are also different perspectives on the concepts expressed by different constituencies. Each partner in a co-op advertisement, each member of a consortium, the flag management company, owners/partners, franchisees, customers, and vendors and suppliers all may have different perspectives. Let's briefly look at the major pros, cons, and areas of concern about each concept. In doing so, we will point out not only the returns but also the risks. For purposes of this analysis, we are intentionally focusing on the application of these concepts in the marketing discipline.

Co-ops

There are numerous benefits to co-oping in the hospitality industry. In fact, it is usually efficient and effective as a marketing tool. Benefits may include stretching your reach, frequency, buying power, and enhancing your product/service offer. This latter benefit can take the form of a more attractive offer, more convenient method of purchase, and even increased awareness and brand image. Certainly being part of an attractive package to a destination that lends itself to packaging, (such as Las Vegas, Hawaii, Florida, etc.) has its advantages. Having your brand available through the distribution and purchasing channels of your co-op partner(s) increases the odds of purchase and offers additional convenience to the consumer and perhaps even larger commissions to the intermediary. Increased awareness comes with increased frequency made possible by the co-operative buying power of the group in the co-op versus one individual entity. In addition, selecting the right co-op partner(s) can also enhance your brands, product or service image.

There are a few pitfalls to look for in co-operative endeavors. First, you may not always be in total control of the effort. A partner, agency, or intermediary may directly interface with your customers. Second, while you may have an equal position on the co-operative programme, your reputation and image could suffer as a result of a partner mishandling a customer or just not living up to your level of service. Third, if you or your agency do not have the lead or control in the co-op, you may not receive your fair share of the endeavor. For example, actual media placement may favor the partner in control of the agency. Responses to calls and leads may be prioritized in favor of your partner, and so forth.

Contributing funds to a co-operative programme, be it programme specific or within a large franchise system or chain can also lead to issues of fairness in how, when, and where funds are allocated, not to mention what the actual promotional message consists of with respect to the offer. Co-mingling of franchise and parent company funds as well as owners and chain management company funds needs to be fair and monitored closely. Not having written agreements, weighting allocated dollars unfairly, or not having complete agreement by all on the offers, terms, and conditions can lead to disgruntled partners or even legal action. There are also numerous ways your overall brand image can be hurt or damaged by non-participation of a franchisee(s) or by partial fulfillment of the co-op offer.

Overall, a well planned and executed co-op with good partners usually produces a positive experience. The risks are lower and the control greater than in a consortium or cluster marketing arrangement.

Consortiums

To some degree consortiums function like a co-op however tend to be more permanent in nature. Consortiums also function like a cluster, where efficiencies in manpower are one driving force. In fact, with consortiums entire functional departments or the majority thereof are replaced by the consortium. In marketing, individual properties as well as chains may opt to have their reservations, group sales, trade show representation, etc., performed by paying a fee or proportionate amount to the consortium. The advantages include reduced overhead, reduced capital expenditures and equipment, and most likely much greater operating efficiencies. These benefits apply to independent properties, groups of properties and to chains. Other benefits may include longer operating hours, substantially more reach (distribution), better training, and customer service.

The downsides for marketing related consortiums include third party interface with customers, not receiving fair treatment (especially smaller participating properties), and the need to feed, nourish and monitor the consortium. Strong oversight is needed with respect to rates/revenue generation, fees charged, and fair share issues. More pitfalls may include the stability of the consortium itself from both a financial and managerial perspective. In the case of a marketing consortium you are trusting a third party with an essential functional area of your business and with handling your up sell, down sell and customer interface at the point of purchase.

Consortiums may make considerable economic sense. In fact, they may be better. more professional and more efficient than either the independents or small chain's own function in this area. An independent management company and flag (chain's) management company may see the same advantages, however, the owner may view the arrangement as less competitive or even inadequate. Would you as an owner want your management company to "farm out" your customer interface and reservations activities? Obviously, not every consortium will live up to expectations. This is especially dangerous for a management company if the property is under performing. It is dangerous for a number of reasons. First, you do not have direct control. Second, it will likely take more time to fix than if it were your own departmental function. Third, the sense of urgency and motivational push is not as great. Fourth, if you decide to switch consortiums or go back and perform the function(s) yourself, more time and investment will be required. One must consider how much time or patience can be expected on the part of owners. If not enough, it is most likely the management contract will be terminated. And, in severe cases, independent hotels might be cash short.

A similar set of benefits and pitfalls exist in other types of consortiums. For example, in the purchasing area the economies of scale and efficiencies may be exceptionally favorable. On the other hand, if your goods do not arrive on time or at all you will really have to scramble to operate. Also, you may sacrifice product customization for quantity and efficiencies, not to mention lack of choice or dominance by major participants if you are the small player.

Clusters

A small or large group of properties may for a cluster in any given market or state. The cluster may be made up of single brand or multiple brands of the same parent company. These properties may be owned, joint-ventures, managed or franchised. Clusters may be formed in a variety of functional areas (i.e., marketing, security, housekeeping, etc.). The common thread is usually the perceived efficiencies and effectiveness of the cluster versus one property.

Cluster marketing is when multiple lodging facilities in a given or like market share their group business leads and inquiries (and sometimes personnel). The decision as to which lodging facility receives a piece of group business may be made by a superimposed "cluster market sales director." This individual is an employee of the chain management company or independent management company.

Let's look closer at how cluster marketing may be organized and function. For this purpose, we will simply designate the "management company" as the XYZ management company. The XYZ management company may have no equity in any of the managed properties or it may hold a percentage equity in one or more properties and even ownership of another in the same "cluster market." The management company may have contracts with several different flag (brands) properties within the common geographical market. In some situations franchise properties may also be included or participate. These properties may not all be of the same quality levels but they all are under managerial direction of the XYZ management company.

The XYZ Company believes that these properties can best be served with an organized "cluster concept" sales and marketing effort. Each property may have its own sales director and various sub-sales managers, but in essence all are part of the XYZ management company. In the simplest form of example, the XYZ management company establishes an unofficial "super sales director" who has responsibility for making sure that business (group meetings, etc.) is "correctly allocated" to the various properties. Thus, the various property sales directors are required to share their leads, their near closings (about to be signed to a contract) business, rate quotes etc., with the super sales directors or cluster leader. The "etc." may include rates, forecasts, and REVPAR projections. This is usually handled through instant access to the computerized data from each cluster property. Weekly meetings are utilized to share more data, provide updates, and often to "direct" business to specific properties. For example, an individual property may have a "hot lead" and be about to "close" on the group when the super sales director may strongly suggest or even direct the specific business to another of the XYZ management companies properties or cluster members in the market that is deemed "more appropriate."

Moreover, an individual property may be told not to call upon a specific prospect because this prospect is more appropriate to another property in the cluster. In some instances, the benefits of cluster marketing may involve cost savings by actually combining select sales functions between properties or consolidating functions at a "mother' or the largest property to handle all others. Obviously, there can be numerous conceptual variations driven by cost efficiencies, elimination of duplicate functions, and overhead reductions. In some cases, the "super sales manager" is a "triad" or small office of three or revenue committee that makes the decisions. Irrespective of the organizational concept, the employees are usually all XYZ management company or the cluster dominated by the XYZ management company.

In an ideal world and assuming the "super sales director" is perceptive and objective there are likely to be a number of substantial benefits to the cluster marketing concept.

There are many common goals and objectives shared by the owner of a lodging facility and the company selected to manage that facility. Perhaps most important of all is the maximization of financial performance of the owner's asset under the care of the management company. The owner seeks the best return of investment possible and the management company seeks the payment of maximum fees (base and incentive). However, there are occasions such as in times of industry downturns where the focus changes to retention of the asset and of the management contracts.

Under this scenario there are pressures to both increase revenue and cash flow as well as to control and reduce expenses and costs. Efficiencies are demanded and often capital improvements deferred. Survival for both the owner and management company becomes preeminent. It is important to understand an owner's perspective not only changes or is influenced by the lodging industry's financial and economic cycles, but also can be influenced by numerous other business and/or personal factors.

Owner's Perspective

Cluster marketing and other like cooperative concepts should be of primary focus for any owner for the simple reason it can have a dramatic impact on the performance and value of the lodging asset. When times are good the focus is usually on maximizing revenue and/or enhancing the value of the lodging asset through capital improvements. When times are bad, the focus shifts to minimizing cost. In this later circumstance an owner may look at cluster marketing as a potential savior. There are some of the major pros perceived to support the cluster concept. These pros provide the owner the positive rationale for cluster participation. They are:

— reduced overhead expenses for sales personnel
— increased lead and group sales generation
— potential movement of business to the owner's property
— potential increased REVPAR by "matching" (higher rated) groups to the owner's property
— larger pool of business (potential)
— "super sales director" expertise and contacts

Bottom line to the owner is cluster marketing has the potential to reduce costs and generate more business and/or a better mix of business. Sounds like a win-win scenario on the surface and it may well be a winner.

However, the owner's perspective should take into consideration a few more things. For example, how many other lodging facilities will be part of the cluster and where will the owner's property fall in terms of priority? What controls are in place to assure a fair allocation of business to the owner's property? Why would the management company place the owner's property as a top priority if the management has no financial interest in the asset or if the management company has substantially more equity in other cluster market facilities? Who will monitor the efforts and how will fairness be achieved?

The answer to many of these questions may well satisfy the owner. Also, the cost savings and potential for incremental revenue may outweigh the concerns. Or, the owner may conclude there are potentially too many risks, and unknowns to go along with the concept. Some simple questions the owner should ask the management company desirous of utilizing cluster marketing include, but are not limited to:

— Will complete access to all data and decisions be readily available to the owner or owner's representative?

— Will there be true cost savings or simply a reallocation of personnel and resources to help all cluster properties with no net savings to the owner's property?

— What fail safe(s) will be put in place to guarantee business (and leads) will not be disproportionately shifted to other properties in which the management company has greater equity?

— Will the owner have input or say on the selection and appointment of the "super sales director" as well as the workings of the marketing cluster?

— What happens to leads, future business, personnel, computer programmes, etc., should the XYZ company management contract be terminated?

— What impact will being part of a cluster marketing group of properties have on the image and resultant real estate value of the owner's asset? How will the owner's lodging facility be positioned (rate, facility, service, etc.) in relationship to other cluster lodging facilities?

— Is the management company (especially chain management company) willing to share all sales data and performance on an equitable basis for all properties in the cluster (including the chain management company's owned properties)? Are other owners of other properties willing to also share the data?

Management Perspective

Independent and flag (chain) hotel management companies perspectives on cluster marketing are largely premised upon two overriding factors. First, the economies of scale favor a group of hotels from the same competitive set and/or market when employing data base marketing as well as a combined group sales effort. Second, the costs incurred in developing and/or acquiring a qualified list of prospective customers (particularly groups) can be spread overall members of the cluster. Also, research efforts may be combined, sales blitzes coordinated, and the general sales effort may be partially consolidated. The net result is substantial savings.

More positive benefits include helping properties to avoid oversells and guest walking and a better match of customer needs to specific properties and resultant customer satisfaction. Other benefits of a cluster include the synergy of common training programmes and sales procedures. The benefits of a cluster for an independent or flag (chain) management company are very strong on their own merits.

However, while the initial perspective on cluster marketing is positive and sounds good, there are a number of pitfalls and concerns. First, the cluster will need to be fair and balanced with respect allocating leads and/or booking business. This means the cluster leader and all related systems must focus on equal treatment for each participant. This can create a natural conflict for the cluster leader as well as others. It raises the question of who or which property receives a profitable piece of business. Assume three properties can all accommodate a highly profitable group with respect to space, availability and rate. The lead/call comes into the "cluster leader" who happens to be the director of sales for a flag/chain owned and managed property. The other properties in the cluster that can handle the business include a chain management contract property and a franchise. Which property receives the business? What mechanism is in place to assure all properties are aware of and have an equal chance to receive the business?

Another pitfall is group business being filtered through a cluster can be a negative experience. In this instance, let's say the only property available for a major customer of the hotels in the cluster is a franchise that also happens to be the lowest ranking in service. The company/group is locked into the franchise property and has a totally unsatisfactory experience. The unsatisfactory experience with the brand (franchise) leads to negative word of mouth about the brand and market. This poor group/guest experience may have a negative effect on the entire cluster and/or brand.

Perhaps the two greatest cautions voiced about cluster marketing relate to the issues surrounding control and pricing. With respect to control, it is simply difficult to give control of your group revenue and large portion of your revenue management to someone else. In the case of a management contract property, this may be particularly sensitive to the owner(s), especially if the hotel is not performing well. With respect to pricing, the cluster concept must be structured and monitored very carefully to assure no laws are broken.

Another focal point often overlooked in cluster marketing is the loyalty, motivation, and incentives related to individual sales personnel. Is one penalized or rewarded for referring business to another property? Is the employee loyal to the cluster, or property to which they were assigned? Many other managerial questions and considerations need to be addressed before joining a cluster or forming a cluster.

Hotel Development Management

DEVELOPING A HOTEL

It is very important to understand the needs of the hotel before even the construction begins. This can be done only by the Facilities Managers, who understands the pre-requisites of a hotel. There are specific needs in the construction of a hotel, mainly Security and Safety needs. Infrastructural requirement in a hotel are different from normal buildings, this includes HVAC, Drainage system, Garbage disposal, Fire alarm, sprinkler system etc. Understanding of these requirements is also very important for opening of a hotel.

Main activities involved in opening of a hotel may be classified as follows:

1. Back office activities.
2. Human Resources Development & Training.
3. Operational Activity.
4. Sales and Marketing Activity.

Back Office Activities

Establishment of a back office, that includes, Finance Department, Purchase Department, Stores/Receiving

Department, Human Resources Department and IT Department. Accounting starts from the day one of the opening activity. Pre-opening activity include preparation of expense budget for pre-opening, procuring materials and storing, choosing of a property management system that suits the hotel, preparation of various policies, procedures and manuals for the operation of the hotel, filling-up of various positions through advertisement and recruitment agencies. Obtaining various licenses and government approvals before opening of a hotel is very important. Financial Controller is the one normally takes the responsibility of Purchase, systems and IT, legal and Stores Department apart from his Finance and Accounting functions in small hotels, however, this differs in large hotels. All the back office activities must be coordinated by the General Manager in the preparation of opening of a hotel.

Human Resources Development & Training

A hotel building may look very beautiful, but, the life is given to the building only by human resources. Human Resources are the biggest asset of any hotel. One has to realize the uniqueness of the hotel industry that lowest paid employee is servicing the highest paid client. Establishment of standards of service is very important. This can be achieved only by developing the existing human resources through training. Getting the right kind of people is the biggest task of Human Resources Department. Due to the scarcity of the required talent, one may have to hire expatriate although they are expensive. Payroll costs are the main ingredient of the total cost in the hospitality industry. Often, the owners would like to know the payroll cost with comparison to the other hotels in the region. Getting right people at right cost at the right time becomes a task for the Human Resources Manager.

Many hotels does not give importance to training as there is a cost involved and they feel employees learn on their own while doing their job. In order to establish a standard, training is the only answer and it has to be continuous. As there is continuous change in all walks of life, in order to satisfy the changing need training is a must. Once the selection is done, next comes the training. Training of personnel has to be done in parity with the standard of service that is expected from them. Each hotel has to set its own standard of service depending on their classification and positioning.

Operations Activity

In every hotel operation, first comes the General Manager and Financial Controller but, many tend to forget a very important position for a new hotel "Chief Engineer". Chief Engineer must be the first person who should be appointed after the General Manager. Chief Engineer will be able to asses and foresee any problems that may arise due to the lack of any facility provided by the property. He will be able to guide the General Manager in rectifying or correcting any problem that may directly affect the guest service in the future.

Next comes, the establishment of other operational heads such as Executive House Keeper, Front Office Manager, Food and Beverage Manager and Executive Chef. These operational heads must make their team in co-ordination with the Human Resources Department and General Manager. All appointments of junior staff must be chosen by the departmental heads and approved by the General Manager.

All Department Heads must be involved in the pre-opening process, such as, training, making budgets and preparation of standard operating procedures (SOP).

They must ensure they have all equipments in place required in their department for smooth operation before opening of a hotel.

Sales and Marketing

Along with the above activities sales and marketing activity must start in parallel. Marketing activity includes focusing on business that includes, making competition analyses, SWOT analysis, positioning of the hotel, establishment of market segments, Advertising and promotion. Director - Sales and Marketing must make his own team of sales personnel who should co-ordinate with him in preparation of Sales Budget and Marketing Plan. Often felt by sales personnel first year budget is bit difficult to prepare as historical data not available. Still an experienced person can easily draw out a sales budget and marketing plan based on the current market trends in the region. Once the sales budget is prepared and approved, expense budget also can be prepared by other department members and sent to Finance for consolidation.

This is a coordinated activity, supervised by the General Manager. Owner need to decide the date of opening well in advance and communicate to the General Manager. Understanding of all the activities becomes very important for successful opening of a hotel.

MASS CUSTOMIZATION

Mass production as a paradigm of management has dominated the world industrial production since World War II, and it has fettered the tremendous growth in American economy in the twentieth century. With shifting demographics and changing consumer tastes and preferences, mass production for homogeneous markets is not enough to keep businesses going. In the present business world, organizations are facing tremendous forces to change to stay ahead of competitors. The companies that responded properly and quickly to changes are now beginning to master a new frontier in business competition. These companies found that not only can higher quality yield lower costs, but so can greater variety. In 1993, Pine stated that:

> "Customers can no longer be lumped together in a huge homogeneous market, but are individuals whose individual wants and needs can be ascertained and fulfilled. Reducing life-cycles and fragmenting demand can yield powerful advantages. Leading companies have created processes for low-cost, volume production of great variety, and even for individually customized goods and services. They have discovered the new frontier in business competition: Mass Customization."

Mass customization is arising in direct response to the turbulence that has splintered the mass market. One sharp-eyed observer who spotted the coming of mass customization long ago is perhaps United States' best known futurist, Alvin Toffler. As far back as 1970, Toffler wrote in Future Shock about "destandarized" goods and services that he forecast the United States would produce in "great variety." Speaking recently to INC by telephone, Toffler said that mass customization will proceed with a kind of gravitational force because, as American become more affluent, they have wanted greater individuality. People now can afford it partly because technology makes it cheaper. Michael Cox, chief economist at the Federal Reserve Bank of Dallas, in concurrence with Toffler lamented that "If you don't customize, you're going to lose business in today's marketplace."

Nowadays, virtually all companies recognize the need to be customer driven by providing superior service to satisfy customers' needs. But as customers and their needs grow increasing diverse, unnecessary cost and complexity are inevitably added to operations. Companies around the world have embraced mass customization in an attempt to avoid those pitfalls of trying to meet every customer's need. Readily available information technology and flexible processes permit them to customize goods or services for individual customers in high volumes and at a relatively low cost. Little has been published in the hospitality and tourism literature about this important production concept.

Mass customization is neither a simple strategy to undertake organizationally and operationally, nor is it a simple concept to comprehend. Hart defined mass customization by using two distinct definitions:

— *The visionary definition*: The ability to provide customers with anything they want profitably, any time they want it, anywhere they want it, any way they want it.

— *The practical definition*: The use of flexible processes and organizational structures to produce varied and often individually customized products and services at the low cost of a standardized, mass production system.

According to Hart, the goal in the first definition will rarely be achieved by an organization. It was considered a transcendent, absolute idea that exists solely as an ideal. The goal in the second definition is not the "anything-at-any-time" promised by the visionary definition. It is "to ascertain, from the customer's perspective, the range within which a given product or service can be meaningfully customized (i.e. differentiated) for that customer, and then to facilitate the customer's choice of options from within that range." He lamented that the concept of producing tailor-made or partially tailor-made goods or services according to customer desire, with very short cycle times and mass production efficiencies, is a more realizable goal than that offered by the visionary definition.

In essence, mass customization is a hybrid technique by which a company churns out products in typical assembly-line fashion yet can add unique features to individual orders. This requires a flexible manufacturing system that anticipates a wide range of options. However, due to the vast differences in customer preferences, mass customization, too, can produce unnecessary cost and complexity. Therefore, it is crucial that managers must examine thoroughly what kind of customization their customers would value before they adopt this new strategy.

Decision Factors

Should companies pursue a mass customization strategy? Hart further identified four key decision factors:

1. *Customer sensitivity.* The first question companies need to ask themselves is: Do your customers care whether you offer more customization? If the answer is no, the mass customization potential is limited.

2. *Process amenability.* This is a multifaceted area. The first obvious question is: Does your process technology, which exists in your area allow you to customize your product or service to individual customers? If it does, the next question is how extensive an overhaul is required to incorporate this technology into your existing process and how much investment will be required? Another part of process amenability is marketing. Since the goal of mass customization is products or services tailored to individual customers, an important question for companies to ask is: Does

the marketing department have access to the level of detail regarding customer needs and the capacity to analyze such information? A third consideration is design. Is your company capable of translating custom needs into actual specifications? The last consideration under this factor is production and distribution. Partly depending on the form and nature of product or service, the flexibility of the production system to handle mass customization is a critical point here.

3. *Competitive environment.* The major question here is: Are there competitive forces that would enhance or detract from the advantage your company would gain from implementing mass customization? In other words, would you be the first in your market with a mass-customized product? How long would it take for competitors to react? And how will your competitors' customers react?

4. *Organizational readiness.* The last decision factor requires an honest assessment of your company's culture and resources. Is your company able and ready to capitalize on the opportunity inherent in mass customization? Organizational change requires enlightened leadership, open-minded management, and financial resources. Hence, mass customization strategy is unique to the company developing and implementing it. There is no "cookie-cutter" approach to creating such a strategy. Mass customization strategy that works for one company might not work for another company.

Approaches to Customization

In 1997, Gilmore and Pine identified four distinct approaches to customization, which are collaborative, adaptive, cosmetic, and transparent. They advocated that when designing or redesigning a product, process, or business unit, managers should choose an approach or a mix of some or all of the four approaches to serve their own particular set of customers.

1. *Collaborative customization.* This approach follows three steps: first to conduct a dialogue with individual customers to help them articulate their needs; second, to identify the precise offering that fulfills those needs; and third, to make customized products for them. Collaborative customization is most appropriate for businesses whose customers cannot easily articulate what they want and grow frustrated when forced to select from a plethora of options.

2. *Adaptive customization.* Adaptive customizers offer one standard, but customizable, product that is designed so that users can alter it themselves. This approach is appropriate for businesses whose customers want the product to perform in different ways on different occasions, and available technology makes it possible for them to customize the product easily on their own.

3. *Cosmetic customization.* This approach is appropriate when customers use a product the same way and differ only in how they want it presented. in other words, the standard offering is packaged specially for each customer.

4. *Transparent customization.* This approach is appropriate when customers' needs are predictable or can easily be deduced, and especially when customers do not want to state their needs repeatedly. Offerings were customized within a standard package for individual customers.

To sum up, collaborative customizers change the product itself in addition to changing some aspect of the presentation while a cosmetic customizer changes only the presentation of the product. A transparent customizer uses a standard representation to mask the customization of the product and finally adaptive customizers change neither the product nor the representation of the product but they provide the customer with the ability to change both the product's function and/or its presentation to meet their needs.

Pioneers of Mass Customization

It is important to look beyond the hospitality industry for ways to mass customize products and services in order to learn from other industries. The following section discusses how some companies in the hospitality industry, as well as other industries mass customized their products and services. First, let's examine a few specific companies and see how they shifted from mass production to mass customization. They are summarized in Table 1.

Table 1. Examples of Paradigm Shift

Companies	Mass customization approach
Dell Computer	Dell Computer uses the collaborative approach and assembles computers to customer's exact specifications. In 1998, Dell sells around 6 million US dollars worth of built-to-order PCs a day. Dell passed IBM in early 1998 to claim the second spot in PC market share.
British Airways	The London-based airline plans to deliver top-notch customer service to its first-class frequent flyers through streamlining its supply-chain process. Understanding passengers' needs beforehand makes it possible for BA to deliver individualized items for passengers on each flight just before takeoff.
Ritz-Carlton	Ritz-Carlton uses software to personalize guests' experience by linking to database filled with quirks and preferences of half a million guests. Any bellhop or desk clerk can find out whether a guest is allergic to feathers, their favorite newspaper, or whether they like extra towels.

The company stores guest information in a database and uses it to tailor the service to each guest on his/her next visit. This is a way to transparently customize for those customers who do not want to be bothered with direct collaboration.

Planters Company	Planters chose cosmetic customization when it retooled its old plant in Suffolk, Virginia. As an example, Wal-Mart wanted to sell peanuts and mixed nuts in larger quantities and 7-Eleven did. In the past, Planters could produce only long batches of small, medium, and large cans giving customers only these few standard packages which may not meet their requirements. Today, Planters can quickly switch between sizes, labels, and shipping containers, responding to each retailer's desires on an order-to-order basis.
Regent, Hong Kong	In the fine dining restaurant, the hotel cosmetically customizes paper napkins and matchbox by printing their customers' name on them. Although personalizing a service in this way is cosmetic, it is of value to many customers.
Lutron Electronics	Lutron's customers can adapt its lighting systems to maximize productivity at the office or to create appropriate moods at home without having to experiment with multiple switches each time they desire a new effect. The customer can quickly achieve the desired effect by punching in the programmed settings.
ChemStation	ChemStation produces industrial soap after independently analyzing each customer's needs. It formulates the right mixture of soap for each customer, which goes into a standard tank. The company learns each customer's usage pattern and delivers more soap before the customer has to ask. This approach eliminates the need for reordering. This is the transparent approach since the customer does not know which soap formulation they have or how much is in inventory but they know the soap works and is always there when they need it.

Fast-Food

Now, let's look more closely into how the hospitality industry mass customized products and services. Much has been said about the standardizing forces of McDonaldization in the wider society. Fast-food restaurants and other McDonaldized systems are mass production systems, which were built upon the belief that in the world of mass production, consumers accept homogeneous products. Their acceptance facilitates market growth and the reduction of prices through economies of scale, which in turn leads to a greater price gap between mass-produced goods and that of customized goods.

As with other mass producers, the fast-food industry has reached the limited of the old paradigm. In 1995, Taylor and Lyon reported mass customization as an alternative to McDonaldization. They recognized that fast-food companies, including McDonald's, have experienced the same sources of discontinuity as other mass producers, creating extreme pressure for change. Burger King was the first one to embrace the principles of mass customization - "Have it your way!" and "Sometimes you've gotta break the rules!" The focus then was on burgers and fries but later shifts testified that this was only the start. Using McDonald's as an example, it can be seen that standardization is still a characteristic of its operations. However, its menu has been expanded not only to suit local tastes and preferences but also to offer more variety. Pizza, fajitas, breakfast burritos, submarine sandwiches, spaghetti and meatballs, carrot and celery sticks were included in some menus.

Internationally, for McDonald's in France the menu is written in three to five different languages, usually, French, German, Italian, Belgian, and Japanese. Some menu items, which are offered in France, are not available in the United States. These items are bagels, red seasoned potato wedges with dipping sauce, cakes and pastries, scones and croissants. The drinks offered are also different. Dr. Pepper and root beer are not offered while Orangina, an orange flavored carbonated drink, beer and wine are available for purchase. For the breakfast menu, McDonald's in France also offers a fruit salad and scones. Salad and dessert choices are also varied, as the chef salad is served with salmon and shrimp, and eclairs, brownies, muffins, and beignets are included in the dessert menu. Pork is not used in Muslim nations. Big Macs in India are prepared with mutton. Soups are offered in Hong Kong operations. Beverage cup sizes are much smaller in Asian countries' McDonald's, and there is no refill.

Lodging

It was pointed out that the hospitality industry has generally preferred to keep wages low, thus avoiding the need for technological innovation, particularly in the actual delivery of its services. Although technology has been used extensively in a supporting role to enhance performance and effectiveness, (e.g., computer reservation system, air control technology, accounting system) there has been a great reluctance to replace human service providers with technologically driven alternatives. However, in recent years, some "tinkering" of mass customization has occurred in selected areas in the lodging industry. Mass customization is made possible by technological applications.

There have been ample discussions about the aging global population and its implications for future marketing strategies and service provisions. This new demographic trend suggests new features in the hotel room that caters specifically to the needs and preferences of the senior travelers. These new features, made possible by technology include:

— ergonomically-designed furniture that facilitates standing from a seated position with the aid of a weight/height sensing cushion or provides support to a tired back through sensors that adjust to the most comforting back support;

— blankets that utilize the same fiber technology as found on the space shuttles heat shield and thus will respond to body temperature retaining or expelling heat to maintain a comfortable temperature and more restful night's sleep;

— alarm clocks that awaken the guest to increasing light levels that begin with the light daybreak to a full daylight, for those whose hearing may riot be as sharp as it was in the past.

The applications of virtual reality are also a unique feature of the future hotel room. The project is examining the applications of video walls that would replace or perhaps supplement windows in guest rooms, allowing the room's occupant to select the scenery that would be most complimentary to her/his activity in the room.

For the business traveler in the work zone it might be sights and sounds that are most stimulating to the busy executive's productivity, transferring to the entertainment zone with sights and sounds from his/her favorite sporting event or concert; and finally to the relaxation/ rest zone, where the stress business traveler can unwind with the sight/sounds of family or a favorite vacation spot.

RETHINKING THE HOTEL BUSINESS ENVIRONMENT

During the past decade, dramatic changes have occurred on all levels in the hotel industry. Eight years of record occupancies, average rates, and profitability were followed by a dramatic drop in occupancy, rate and profitability. During that period, technology advanced to the stage that, now, business is conducted almost exclusively with computers, cell phones, and palm pilots, and can be orchestrated as effortlessly in the back seat of a cab— anywhere in the world— as in an office!

The cost effectiveness of technology, coupled with its global reach, has contributed to the new hotel environment. With the encouraging business outlook, hotels are now, more than ever, in a position to assess the new business environment and to establish a strategic business plan which incorporates these changes and are designed to grow and adapt to changing market conditions.

Technology has brought numerous advantages to conducting business, including servicing existing customers and in reaching new markets. But as a service industry, it is important to ensure that technology is used to enhance guest satisfaction, especially in the case of free-standing boutique hotels. One key factor that differentiates boutique hotels from large or chain affiliated hotels is its personalized service.

Therefore, in order to benefit from the many applications of technology (i.e. reducing expenses, generating demand, and increasing guest satisfaction), and to simultaneously maintain the personalized services characteristic of boutique hotels, it is important for owners and managers to re-think and evaluate the following key areas:

Web Marketing

Regardless of the size of the marketing budget, the Web has evolved into the most important component of the marketing plan. Properly developed, executed, and maintained, the Web will, at a minimum cost, effectively reach local, domestic, and international markets. It is especially important to understand the difference between the two key components, i.e. the artistry of the design and the technology, and how to integrate the two. Many times, Web sites are created by technology professionals who do not understand the nuances of marketing; and vice versa, marketing professionals who design a Web site only from a visual perspective, without consideration of how key technical components, built in, can drive demand.

An effective Web site design and effective an on-line distribution strategy require expertise. The lay person is bombarded with many ideas and is left wondering which approach to take. Therefore, if relying on expert advice, it is important to have a customized plan to accomplish specific short term goals, as well as ensure that the Web site is well positioned for future technological advances and for advancements with the search engines, in order to minimize financial risks.

With the growth of the Web, there are many parties creating ways to profit. Search engines, third party internet booking companies, and advertisers, to name a few, all have competitors, so they are ever-evolving in order to dominate the market and to increase their own businesses. Therefore, before going forward with a plan and to spend wisely, it is necessary to fully understand all of the options and choose the best ones for your short term as well as long term goals.

Reservations

Just a few years ago, new technology helped owners and operators reduce expenses and create demand by centralizing reservations and providing a toll free number for customers. Now, with the new technological advancements coupled with new customer buying habits, the industry has evolved to using "on-line" and "off-line" reservations as part of its daily vocabulary. Booking on-line reduces costs by reducing labor, but the key is to provide the information and service that will allow and encourage the customer to book and generate revenues! If the information is not there to help the customer make a decision or if it is not easy to book a reservation, business will be lost.

A small, boutique hotel can benefit from the advanced technology allowing customers to book directly on-line, using the Web site. Planning and maintenance is the key, which can only be done by people exercising good judgment, not technology. Therefore, to maximize the on-line booking capabilities, designate a staff member to ensure that rates, promotions, and room inventory are consistently up to date, and that the customer has the ease of booking, revising, and canceling. A simple process of trying many hotel Web sites will help identify the elements which make a great reservations system from a customer's perspective.

Guest Interaction

In many ways, technology has created an impersonal way of doing business. But, we all benefit from the convenience it brings to our lives and enjoy the option of doing business 24/7 by using the Internet, e-mail, voice mail, text messaging, etc. We can order products and services from all over the world and have immediate access to information by just pushing a button! But keeping in mind that personal service generally distinguishes the small independent hotel from the large chains, it is important to evaluate the areas of guest interaction and measure the impact of technology. The personal touch of interacting with guests and potential guests in a warm, efficient, and professional manner, either over the phone or in person, is a powerful tool that fosters goodwill and guest loyalty, which translates to market share and revenues.

By fully exploiting the product distinctions of small boutique hotel and using technology wisely, owners and managers are well positioned to compete against the large chains to impact market share, minimize expenses, and generate profitability.

PITFALLS IN HOTEL DEVELOPMENT

Cost overruns and construction delays can easily turn a profitable project into a development nightmare, of ten losing millions of dollars in the process. The careful selection and engagement of a professional Project and Development Services manager who represents the owner's best interests will be the most valuable project cost allocation made in a hotel development. In this section some of the pitfalls encountered in hotel development are describes.

Building A Dream Rather Than A Financial Winner

Issue

Historically, many hotels were developed as trophy assets, often with little regard to the underlying economics of the development. While these types of developments were common in the late 1980s, they have by in large become the exception today.

The first question that needs to be asked is why build a new hotel. The answers will range from financial to fantasy.

The first step in any development process is to "prove" the vision; the most successful hotel developers set aside a judicious amount of time in the development cycle to validate their ideas.

Solution

The first and indispensable step of a project delivery process is the confirmation of the owner's goals and objectives. Even if they have already been established, a thorough review of the goals and objectives is appropriate when a development team is retained. Constraints should be investigated to assure all budget and schedule risks are exposed. Objectives for image and costs must be tested in the market to assure expectations can be met. The owner's decision-making process, financing requirements and similar concerns will be explored to unearth unforeseen risks.

Project planning, including the selection of all consultants, needs to be reviewed and coordinated from the beginning. The financial objectives of the development need to be established and clearly communicated, including the holding strategy, return on investment, equity available and the likelihood of raising construction and long-term financing.

As a development team will be responsible for the implementation of the owner's decisions made early in the process, it is beneficial to introduce the development manager early in the development cycle to avoid divergent agendas of architects, contractors, operators and owners.

Having The Wrong Entity Driving The Process

Issue

Very early in the development process, the owner must form their team. This team includes the owner, developer, architect, engineer, interior designer as well as other consultants unique to the project such as contractors, attorneys, financial advisers, appraisers and operators. Usually, there are three drivers jockeying for the lead position: the owner, the developer and the operator. All believe they have legitimate reasons for why they should spearhead the project.

Developers assume they should take the lead because they know how to convert the vision into a building. Operators think they should run the show because the hotel must be built according to specifications of their brand. Owners presume they should be in charge because their capital is financing the project. Although the team is assembled based on the owner's concept, the developer and the operator each has a tendency to craft the agreement in a way that allows minimum interference from the owner.

The fact of the matter is that the owner should drive the process at all times/and should be the ultimate decision-maker. After all, the owner is the risk taker and without his or her financial support, the project might remain on the drawing board. This does not mean that the owner should be involved in every detail of the project. Rather, it is assumed that the owner would have selected a competent project team and negotiated with the best suitable operator for the property.

Solution

To ensure the owner's best interests, it is wise to assemble a development team with experience in completing complex hotel projects that can objectively oversee the development activity of a third party. To ensure a timely and successful delivery of a project, a qualified development adviser should initiate the following related processes that are critical to any development.

Pre-construction
- Project Planning
- Capital/Financial Plan Development
- Design Team Selection/Design Management Plan
- Pre-Construction Services and/or General Contractor Selection
- Governmental & Regulatory Requirements
- Hotel Operations Planning & Asset Management Approach
- Schedule & Budget Management Systems
- Bid and Negotiation Services
- FF&E Design, Procurement & Installation Planning

Construction
- Contract Administration, Management Control & Reporting
- Project Coordination & Conflict Resolution
- Budget & Schedule Control
- Change Order Administration
- Quality & Safety Control
- Invoice Approval/DrawPreparation/Cash Flow Management/Reporting
- FF&E Procurement & Phased Installation
- Preparation for Occupancy and Hotel Management Start-up
- Project Close-Out & Operations Turnover

Form At The Expense of Function

Issue

Unlike other types of real estate, the development of a

hotel is the creation of a new business entity. Design decisions made early in the development process stay with the property for its lifetime and can become an operations benefit or nightmare. Decisions about technology, room size, meeting facilities, flexibility with current brand standards, and the mix of food and beverage must be the driving force in "future-proofing" a design so that the property remains competitive well into its future.

Solution

In order to achieve maximum value as well as budget control, a development team needs to ensure that a comprehensive construction estimate and updated project budget is prepared at the end of each design phase (conceptual, schematic, design development and construction documents). This process results in constant checks of the evolving design versus the project budget, which allows issues to be addressed while there is still time to adjust the design or the budget.

Throughout a project, a systematic value engineering approach needs to be adopted to maximize the cost/benefit impact of every dollar invested in the project. The goal of value engineering is to analyze every opportunity, recommendation or new technology/material during the design and construction phase that has the potential to "enhance" the project while maintaining budget and schedule control. Value enhancement can occur (1) when a project can be constructed more economically and efficiently from a cost and schedule standpoint; (2) when new products or more durable material is developed that will decrease operations and maintenance costs, and (3) when operators provide input on functionality, work flow and overall building performance.

The discipline of value engineering requires the evaluation of everything against a pre-determined set of criteria, which are established in the initial development phase with the owner.

Local And Regional Civic Participation

Issue

A hotel should ultimately be developed because it is financially sound and provides the type and quality of services that the market desires. By developing a hotel, the owner is contributing a tangible asset to a local community by providing additional tax revenue and gainful employment. In exchange for these benefits to the community, an owner/developer should take advantage of its privileged position and get support from the local government.

Although not always available, this support can take various forms, from building the access infrastructure (such as an access road to the hotel site) to tax incentive financing. The key is to ensure that all forms of available incentives are investigated and incorporated into the financial plan, if they are favorable to the owner's overall goals and objectives.

Solution

During early due diligence on the project and the site, the owner/developer needs to be familiar with potential public incentives in the municipality where the project will be built. With the right approach, a developer can often obtain financial support from the local and federal government for the project. Following are a few of the options an owner/developer should consider:

— Municipal tax free bonds
— Access infrastructure improvements
— Tax incentive financial (TIF) districts
— Federal historical tax credits
— Environmental clean-ups
— Beach restorations

Limited Contractor Accountability

Issue

Hotel projects are notorious for last minute installations of case goods and scrambles to complete interior finishes. The final push toward the opening deadline of ten forces contractors to cut corners to avoid financial penalties or liquidated damages for missed deadlines. Without defined project controls, the keys to the hotel are often handed to the hotel manager, only to find substandard materials and workmanship that create operating problems well after the contractors have moved onto their next project.

Solution

A comprehensive quality control programme is the backbone to any hotel development and should focus on three primary goals:

(1) knowledgeable design phase input,
(2) clear communication of expectations to contractors, and
(3) regular on-site inspections to review the construction and conformance to the quality standards contained in the design specification and, if necessary, formulate an aggressive programme to correct non-complying work.

As the project progresses, continual reviews of each phase of the project will minimize the final punch list and turnover process so project closeout can be expedited and hotel operations can proceed with minimal interference.

During the final phases of the project, it is imperative to coordinate the efforts of the general contractor and the local authorities to gain all necessary licenses and permits required to open the hotel in conjunction with the hotel operations plan.

The entire project team must be aligned to the goal of opening the hotel on time, with minimal remaining punch list items at the time of turnover to operations. Preliminary and final punch list procedures must be established early in the project to allow sufficient time for completion prior to turnover.

Prior to the expiration of all project warranties, inspections must be conducted to determine the existence of any warranted defects and arrange with the respective manufacturers and subcontractors to correct the defects prior to the expiration of the warranty.

Functional Obsolescence

Issue

Now more than ever, hotel guests are being exposed to ever increasing service levels, design innovations and new technology. Hotel guests are traveling more frequently and are being exposed on a regular basis to the latest in hotel trends and gadgetry. The process of one-upsmanship is nothing new, but to build a hotel today without consideration of future trends may create an asset that soon loses value through functional obsolescence. The mega trends in the lodging industry continue to evolve. We are seeing a continued shift toward quality not quantity, such as the proliferation of boutique hotels offering a unique experience over the cookie cutter approach to corporate lodging. With this evolving landscape, it becomes important to the long-term profitability of a project that every effort is made to incorporate product flexibility in the initial design.

Solution

The time frame on large projects from conception to completion can take anywhere from two to four years. This time frame is a lifetime in terms of technology and means that the available technology, materials and techniques at the start of a project can be vastly different from those available at completion.

To ensure that the "latest thinking" is brought to bear on a given project, it is important to draw from global experience on asset management, project management and financing. It is critical to balance the financial objectives of the project with the overall financial objectives of the asset during operations.

Additionally, as stated previously, the discipline of value engineering will ensure that new technology, materials, products and design changes will be constantly evaluated against the overall design parameters and incorporated into the project should an overall benefit be substantiated.

Back-Door Procurement

Issue

The procurement process needs to be expertly managed and tightly controlled until the last towel is placed in the guestrooms. The hotel FF&E procurement process is full of stories of kickbacks, inferior products being delivered late or the wrong product arriving at the last minute. The procurement process is a haven for cost padding and political and self-serving decisions that affect the hotel operations for the useful life of the products.

Solution

Cost control and quality can be maintained by implementing a coordinated FF&E procurement process including:

— Establishing the RFP process for procurement & installation providers and controlling the process all the way through.

— Challenging the interior designer, the procurement company and the vendors to evaluate and recommend best-in-class solutions to FF&E.

— Reviewing product data and samples proposed with the owner and the hotel operator to make sure they are in compliance with the client 's requirements.

— Developing a plan and coordinating the installation of FF&E in conjunction with the contractor's construction turnover schedule and the operator's training schedules on all elements of the project, including furniture delivery strategies and inventory security.

Costs Spiraling out of Control

Issue

Without a clearly conceived strategy for implementing the project, together with experience, coordination and communication, a project can literally spin out of control. The financial implications that result from development pitfalls can be devastating. Following are some of the potential hazards:

— Labor disputes
— Legal disputes
— Less than ironclad agreements with general contractors and trades, allowing for uncapped price fluctuation
— Accumulation of delays, causing loss of business and increased construction costs
— Accumulation of change orders due to a flawed or incomplete design prior to construction
— Construction conflicts adding to delays
— Lack of contractor/trade warranties
— Non-bonded contractors and trades on the job
— Uncooperative neighbors
— Potential loss of business and goodwill

The business of building a hotel from the ground up is complex and multifaceted. Of ten owners and developers do not account for cost overruns, which can have dramatic implications on the project.

Solution

Experience is key to the hotel development process and qualified advisers can mitigate most of these issues with minimum involvement by the owner. The primary objective of advisers is to ensure that the owner's best interest is met during all stages of development. To accomplish such a project, the development team must focus on the following:

1. Establishing benchmarks and performance targets:

　　— Assembling a design and construction team of best-in-class providers;

— Maximizing the buying power of each dollar spent on the project by testing, evaluating and expanding local contractor and subcontractor relationship negotiations to take advantage of current market conditions and discounts; and

— Challenging design solutions to ensure optimum value for construction dollars and efficient and economical future flexibility.

2. Bringing market leverage and pressure to all cost categories.

3. Mitigating risk and liability.

4. Retaining a high level of control:

— The control of a project's schedule is essential to minimize cost overruns. Process control, scheduling and project management cost reporting systems put real cost containment into the hands of the project team and owner management.

— Expert management provides important initial feasibility information and manages the design and construction process to the interests of the owner. This will produce an end result that is consistent with the overall project goals and business plan.

Overlooking Small Details

Issue

Finally the hotel is built and almost ready to open for business. Often this is when the owner must feverishly scramble to secure all licenses and permits necessary to open the hotel. Time is money, and any delay in the hotel opening can be costly. Construction delays are one aspect of the equation. The other side of the equation is the lack of understanding and knowledge of the process for obtaining the necessary permits, licenses and certificates to open a hotel. The following list represents some of the required licenses and permits prior to opening:

— City Occupational Licenses

— County Occupational Licenses

— Certificate of Registration—Collection of Sales & Use Tax

— Business License (Rooms, Miscellaneous)

— Food & Beverage (Bars/Restaurants)

— Food & Beverage (Kitchens/Food prep areas)

— Beverage Licenses

— Special Tax Stamp

— Swimming Pool Permits

— Elevator/Escalator Certificates of Operation

— Certificate of Balcony Inspection

— Boiler Certifications

— Certification of Fire Protection System

— Fuel Storage Tank Licenses

— Dry Cleaning System Permits

Solution

There is no excuse for not having all the licenses, certificates and permits in place upon completion of the development. These documents may require planning months in advance and should be an integral part of the development's critical path planning. To ensure a smooth process of attaining the necessary licenses and permits, it is important to remain in constant contact with the local government agency throughout the various development phases of the project. Issues are addressed during regular visits with the local inspectors and, therefore, do not accumulate over time to the point that they become unmanageable. Lack of communication translates into licensing delays.

Missing the Deadline

Issue

Project delays resulting in the postponed opening of a hotel can have many adverse consequences. In order to ease the financial pressure of the typical hotel start up, the sales and marketing team will begin to book association and group business 12 to 18 months prior to opening. The importance of establishing an opening date and completing the hotel on schedule is critical to avoid the cost of relocating group bookings and the associated negative publicity. The same can be said for the various publications and directories catering to the corporate and leisure travelers. If group business cannot be layered in and publications and promotional material do not accurately reflect a hotel's opening, the hotel opening is likely to produce poor financial results.

Solution

Critical path planning and adherence to development schedules are imperative to a hotel project's financial success. Managing the development schedule and assuring compliance requires that all interaction between the owner/developer, the hotel operator and the design and construction team are managed.

Management of the development schedule requires an intimate understanding of the owner's decision-making processes, the creation of interim milestone dates with the necessary tracking process, and the necessary expertise to provide real time solutions to remedy construction delays.

To ensure that a hotel opens on time, many construction contracts will include performance clauses such as bonus incentives for early completion or liquidated damages as a penalty for late completion. Other steps that can be implemented to ensure timely openings include staged occupancy of critical components of the hotel. Typically kitchens, training facilities, computer rooms, and laundry and operating supply areas are brought online three to four months before opening, while guest rooms, front office and reception are turned over four to six weeks ahead of opening.

The strict management of the development schedule, including establishing and tracking critical milestones, managing an "Action Item List" throughout design and construction and identifying and tracking long-lead items will result in a smooth ending of a long and demanding development process.

PARTNERSHIP AND OUTSOURCING

Outsourcing happens when a company determines specific tasks are better and more efficiently performed by a provider outside the company that specializes in that particular field. For most companies, cost savings is the main reason for outsourcing. Outsourcing is usually a profitable option when outside providers are more efficient or better able to achieve economies, are capable of reducing over-head or debt, or are able to save on the cost of benefits and administration.

While cost savings is the main reason for outsourcing, it is clearly not the only reason. Outsourcing enables a company to benefit from the knowledge base of the outsource company, which can often provide expertise on complex business issues and processes that are not among the firm's own core competencies. By using outside professionals, management can focus on issues related to growth of the core business.

In the administrative/ finance areas, the functions most frequently outsourced are payroll, tax compliance, internal auditing, accounting and human resources/ hiring. Internal operations primarily in the areas of manufacturing, processing and assembly are outsourced by almost half of the fast growth firms surveyed. Outside maintenance and equipment services are used by 19 percent, and information technology outsourcing is used by 17 percent; up eight full points from three years ago. Sales and marketing are a rapidly growing outsourcing category as well; up nine points in three years. Web site management, a new outsourcing category; is used by 11 percent of fast growth companies.

Partnering promotes a win-win situation for both companies. Instead of paying an out-side vendor to merely perform a task for a fee, partnering puts two companies with differing strengths together to create something much bigger Something along the lines of "the whole being greater than the sum of its parts". Each company brings a level of expertise, or distinction, that benefits the other. Both companies grow and create a better product or service jointly than they could have done individually.

More than half of America's fastest growth companies have partnered with other companies over the past three years to improve existing product lines or devel-op new products or services for an already existing marketplace. In Coopers & Lybrand's study, typical growth firms over the past year were found to have participated in over six partnering arrangements each, resulting in significantly higher growth rates, larger revenues, more innovative products and greater productivity. Overall, more service sector growth firms have been involved in partnering over the past three years than ever before. Especially high levels of partnering were noted among computer-related services and consultants.

While with outsourcing the prime motivation is cost savings, the real payoff of partnering is not necessarily to reduce expenses. The four major benefits of partnering are

— increased sales of existing products

— improved competitive position

— more new products or lines of business created and

— better operations or technology

Partnering can be seen in myriad functions: research; licensing; sharing resources, employees or lab facilities; exchanging information; and educational workshops and seminars. Other cooperative arrangements involve colleges or universities.

Of primary importance to companies involved in partnering is the ability to achieve significant breakthroughs in innovation and creative marketing. Partnering companies collaboratively spend more resources on new product development while focusing more on bigger opportunities and innovation. These partnering pioneers' are on the cutting edge of their industries and won't hesitate to go outside their own organizations to develop relationships with others in the development of their innovative new products.

Bibliography

Angelo, Rocco M. *An Introduction to Hospitality Today*. Orlando: Educational Institute, American Hotel & Motel Association, 1998.

Boni, G. de and Frederick Francis Sharles. *Hotel organization, management and accountancy. Hotel organization and management*. London New York: Sir I. Pitman, 1926.

Boomer, Lucius Messenger. *Hotel management; principles and practice*. New York: Harper, 1931.

Clarenbach, Ernst. *Clarenbach's hotel accounting*. Chicago, Ill.: Hotel monthly press, 1930.

Dicksee, Lawrence Robert. *Hotel accounts*. London: Gee & Co., 1905.

Eckert, Fred William and Howard L. Dayton. *The hotel lease; a study of the business elements and principles involved in making leases that are equitable to both lessee and lessor*. Chicago: Hotel Monthly Press, 1947.

Gray, Madeline and Vass De Lo Padua. *How to be a success in the restaurant business*. Chicago: Nelson-Hall, 1948.

Hamilton, Francis Frazee. *Hotel front desk management, a treatise on the best methods and procedures in use in small hotels*. Miami, Fla.: Francis Frazee Hamilton, 1947.

Hitz, Ralph and National Hotel Management Co. *Standard practice manuals for hotel operation*. New York: Harper, 1936.

Holmes, F. H. *Hotel training course*. Chicago: F.H. Holmes, 1937.

Horwath, Ernest B. and Louis Toth. *Hotel accounting, including departmental control, food costing, and auditing*. New York: The Ronald press company, 1928.

Hotel Management Clipping Bureau of Good Ideas. *Hotel Management Clipping Bureau of Good Ideas*.New York: Ahrens Pub. Co., 1931.

Odell, Margaret K. and Earl Poe Strong. *Records management and filing operations*. New York: McGraw-Hill Book Co., 1947.

Ogden, Henry N. and Henry Burdett Cleveland. *Practical methods of *sewage disposal for residences, hotels and institutions.* New York: J. Wiley, 1912.

Palmer, Mary E. *Guide to hotel housekeeping.* Charleston W Va: The Tribune printing co., 1908.

Pixley, Francis William. *Clubs and their management.* New York: Sir I. Pitman, 1914.

Radell, Neva Henrietta. *Accounting and food control for home economics students.* New York: F.S. Crofts & co., 1935.

Robson, Barbara Reid. *House management problems of fraternities and sororities; an investigation of the supervision or assistance given by educational institutions to fraternities and sororities in their house management problems.* New York city: Teachers college Columbia university, 1933.

Searing, Fred. *Profit building ideas for food and food service.* Stanford, Conn.: Dahl Pub. Co., 1947.

Van Hoof, Hubert B. *A Host of Opportunities: An Introduction to Hospitality Management.* Chicago: Irwin, 1996.

Virts, William B. *Purchasing for Hospitality Operations.* East Lansing: Educational Institute of the American Hotel and Motel Association, 1996.

Walker, John R. *Introduction to Hospitality.* Upper Saddle River: Prentice Hall, 1996.

Ware, Richard. *How to Open Your Own Restaurant: A Guide for Entrepreneurs.* New York: Penguin Books, 1991.

Woods, Robert H. *Quality Leadership and Management in the Hospitality Industry.* East Lansing: Educational Institute of the American Hotel & Motel Association, 1996.

Index